Epidemic of Joy
A Study of Acts 13—16

Studies in Acts by Randal Denny

Do It Again, Lord: Acts 1—4
Where the Action Is: Acts 5—8
Wind in the Rigging: Acts 9—12
Epidemic of Joy: Acts 13—16

Epidemic of Joy

A Study of Acts 13—16

by
Randal Earl Denny

Wipf & Stock
PUBLISHERS
Eugene, Oregon

Wipf and Stock Publishers
199 W 8th Ave, Suite 3
Eugene, OR 97401

Epidemic of Joy
A Study of Acts 13 to 16
By Denny, Randal Earl
Copyright©1988 Paich, Ruth Denny
ISBN 13: 978-1-55635-386-4
ISBN 10: 1-55635-386-3
Publication date 3/26/2007
Previously published by Beacon Hill Press, 1988

Dedication

To Thelma Denny and Bea Gladden
Gene and Bette Smee
Sam and Jo Ann Trett
and
Ray and Evelyn Morton
Who invested in my ministry
When I stood at the crossroads

Contents

Foreword

The name Randal Denny has become well known among ministers in our church. Many preachers long to have their sermons published and quite a few put forth effort to get this accomplished. Few succeed. Randal Denny is an exception. We all look forward to any new volume of sermons from this busy pastor because he has established his reputation as a communicator. We know that new and fresh material is going to be available for us. And this is Rev. Denny's desire. He wants to help other preachers develop homiletical skills as well as constantly improve his own.

But these are not just sermons for preachers. This book also provides inspirational and devotional reading for a wider audience that includes the laity of the church. His expositions on the Book of Acts are wonderful resource material for Sunday School teachers and Bible study leaders. Indeed I have referred to him as the William Barclay of the Church of the Nazarene.

Recently I visited the author in his study and was impressed by his library, as well as his personal discipline in sermon preparation. How fortunate we are that he is able to share all of that with us in this continuing series from the Acts of the Apostles.

In each generation it seems as though the Holy Spirit raises up those among us who have special talents for writing. How fortunate we in this generation are to have the benefit of Randal Denny's able pen. May this book be as great a blessing to those who read it as the reading of the manuscript was to me. I predict the germ thoughts expressed in this sermon series will be repeated from many pulpits throughout the land. If that happens, Randal Denny will feel his purpose in writing will have been fulfilled.

JERALD D. JOHNSON

Preface

Joy to the world! the Lord is come;
Let earth receive her King!

Isaac Watts, who penned those words, was a recipient of the good news of Jesus. We who sing them year after year are indebted to a long chain of men and women who passed along the words of joy. Joseph Marmion exclaimed, "Joy is the echo of God's life within us!"

"Joy is distinctly a Christian word," said Samuel Dickey Gordon. "It is the reverse of happiness. Happiness is the result of what happens of an agreeable sort. Joy has its springs deep down inside. And that spring never runs dry, no matter what happens. Only Jesus gives that joy. He had joy, singing its music within, even under the shadow of the cross."

The homespun evangelist Billy Sunday declared, "If you have no joy in your religion, there's a leak in your Christianity somewhere."

The joy of new life in Christ, scattered from Jerusalem by the advent of persecution, sprang up in distant cities. In Antioch the sparks of joy fanned into flames. The church grew. God expanded their vision of His kingdom until they laid their hands on Barnabas and Saul and sent them across land and sea to tell about Jesus Christ. The Book of Acts describes the epidemic of joy that spread everywhere—until it reaches us today!

Missionary E. Stanley Jones noted, "A strange, sober joy went across that sad and decaying world—joy that goodness was here for the asking, that moral victory was possible now, that guilt could be lifted from the stricken conscience, that inner conflict could be resolved . . . and that a Fellowship of like-souled persons gave one a sense of belonging. It was Good News. And it worked!"

Acts 13 through 16 trace the beginnings of that "epidemic of joy!"

11

Acknowledgments

The congregational family of the Spokane Valley Church of the Nazarene has been infected with the "epidemic of joy!" Their lives, their ministries, their fellowship, and their friendships with me have given evidence that they have "caught the real thing!" To preach to this alive and joyful flock three times every Sunday is high privilege and pure joy. I am indebted to their continuing encouragement and challenge. Now I understand more fully Paul's word, "May the Lord show mercy to the household of Onesiphorus, because he often refreshed me" (2 Tim. 1:16).

Appreciation is hereby expressed for permission to quote from copyrighted material as follows:

Fleming H. Revell Company: William Sanford LaSor, *Great Personalities of the New Testament;* Bishop Festo Kivengere, *I Love Idi Amin.*

Regal Books, a division of G/L Publications: Jerry Cook, *Love, Acceptance and Forgiveness.*

Victor Books, a division of SP Publications: Henry Jacobsen, *The Acts Then and Now.*

Zondervan Publishing House: Clyde M. Narramore, *This Way to Happiness;* Stuart Briscoe, *Living Dangerously.*

I owe a great debt to my wife, Ruth, for the hours writing takes away from our homelife, and to my competent staff who enable me to do my task of preparation: Janice Scheibe, David Cox, Steve Pace, Kim Nielsen, and G. Donald Craker.

RANDAL EARL DENNY
Spokane Valley Church
Spokane, Wash.

1

Handpicked for Greatness

Acts 12:25—13:12

One fellow said, "My psychiatrist tells me that I'm afraid of success, but he says I have nothing to worry about."

Our old world tries to push us down into mediocrity. God's Word says, however: "Don't let the world around you squeeze you into its own mould, but let God re-make you so that your whole attitude of mind is changed. Thus you will prove in practice that the will of God's good, acceptable to him and perfect" (Rom. 12:2, Phillips).

Jesus speaks to the hero in every man's soul. Confident of our capacity for greatness, He beckons, "Follow me." God has handpicked each of us for greatness. Acts 13 unfolds God's plan, which Jesus outlined at His Ascension in Acts 1. His followers would witness in Jerusalem and Judea, then to Samaria, and third, on to the ends of the earth. By the end of Acts 12, the message of Jesus in Judea and Samaria is history. The third stage is launched in Acts 13 and is in progress yet today!

The church at Antioch dominates the Book of Acts from chapter 13 to the end of Acts. The Antioch church was creative and bold. The torch of evangelism passed on to these Christians who were eager to communicate the good news of

13

Jesus. When it came to evangelizing Gentiles, Antioch Christians didn't know it couldn't be done! Evangelism still requires Christians unencumbered by entrenched traditions and long-engrained "religious" habit patterns to get the job done.

In the late 1800s Bishop Wright believed it was impossible for man to fly. He said, "Flight is reserved for the angels." Naturally, Bishop Wright did not invent the airplane—but his two sons, Wilbur and Orville, did. Believing was necessary for it to happen!

"In the church at Antioch there were prophets and teachers" (v. 1). An interesting list of men follows, portraying the universal appeal of the Good News: Barnabas—a Jew from the island of Cyprus; Lucius from North Africa, believed by some to be Luke, author of Luke and Acts; Simeon, a Jew of Roman culture adopting the Roman name Niger; Manaen, raised with Herod Antipas who murdered John the Baptist; and Saul from Tarsus, at about 44 years of age.

Put on the shelf for several years, Saul was brought by Barnabas to Antioch. Meanwhile, God had been preparing Saul. Saul must have felt like Winston Churchill upon his selection as prime minister of Great Britain. All his life had been a preparation for this hour! Abraham Lincoln once said, "I'll study and get ready, and then maybe my chance will come." If you're not prepared and ready, you probably won't recognize opportunity when it comes.

The prophets and teachers in Antioch "were worshiping the Lord and fasting" (v. 2). Engrossed in working together in the Scriptures and prayerfully listening to God, the Holy Spirit revealed His direction for them: "Set apart for me Barnabas and Saul for the work to which I have called them" (v. 2). As a result, Barnabas and Saul launched the first great missionary tour. They traveled in Asia Minor, a peninsula about two-thirds the size of Texas, now known as Turkey.

14

This passage of Acts is more than religious history. As God called, sent, and filled Barnabas and Saul for their mission, He calls, sends, and fills us by His Spirit for ministries of service. We, too, have been handpicked for greatness.

A friend invited Anton Rubinstein, the 19th-century Russian pianist and composer, to go to church with him. He replied, "I will—if you can take me to a church where I will be tempted to achieve the impossible!"

What a challenge! God has, indeed, handpicked us for greatness.

We Are Called by the Holy Spirit

"The Holy Spirit said, 'Set apart for me Barnabas and Saul for the work to which I have called them'" (v. 2).

Like Barnabas and Saul, we are called by *God*. The Bible speaks of "encouraging, comforting and urging you to live lives worthy of God, who calls you into his kingdom and glory" (1 Thess. 2:12). Jesus emphasized, "You did not choose me, but I chose you and appointed you to go and bear fruit—fruit that will last" (John 15:16). God has picked us out for greatness! He calls us to come and serve where He is—elbow deep in human need. God singles us out for His use!

Like Barnabas and Saul, we are *chosen* by God. The Church is the "ecclesia"—the "called-out ones." Paul declared, "For he chose us in him before the creation of the world to be holy and blameless in his sight. In love he predestined us to be adopted as his sons through Jesus Christ, in accordance with his pleasure and will" (Eph. 1:4-5). A child born into a family is accepted, but an adopted child is chosen, selected. We have been adopted or chosen into God's family. In Paul's day, Roman law dictated that an adopted son was more legally secure than a natural son. A natural son could be disinherited, but not the chosen and adopted son. God has picked you out for greatness!

15

Like Barnabas and Saul, we are *endorsed* by God's people. "So after they had fasted and prayed, they placed their hands on them and sent them off" (v. 3). God had commanded, "Set apart for me Barnabas and Saul." Actually the church cannot "ordain." God calls and ordains. The church can only endorse God's man or woman just as the church endorsed Barnabas and Saul and sent them on assignment.

As each person seeks to do God's bidding, the church must wisely and discerningly endorse and encourage each one's God-given ministry. By the laying on of hands, the Antioch church was saying, "Barnabas and Saul, we recognize your unique spiritual gifts assigned by the Holy Spirit. We appoint you to go on behalf of the Christian community. You do not serve alone. We stand with you. You represent us all."

"They . . . sent them off," meaning literally, "They let them go." As we recognize someone's spiritual gift or ministry, we need to "let them go." Each one deserves to be set free to serve under the power of the Holy Spirit. So often we tie each other down with old ways of doing things, with procedural red tape, with our preconceived ideas of how things ought to be done, until ofttimes we squeeze the spontaneity and joy out of ministry. Let's set each other free to serve God unhindered by man-made restraints, for we are called by the Holy Spirit.

We Are Sent by the Holy Spirit

"The two of them, sent on their way by the Holy Spirit, went down to Seleucia and sailed from there to Cyprus" (v. 4). "Sent . . . by the Holy Spirit"—the word *missionary* from the Latin means exactly the same as the Greek word for "apostle"—"one who is sent." Each one of us is sent by the Holy Spirit. He directs God's work. As Commander in Chief, He organizes every campaign. Our marching orders come from Him. Are you the missionary—the sent one—to your circle of the world?

16

Like Barnabas and Saul, we are *sent* from our place of instruction and worship. Going 15 miles downriver, they sailed from the port city, Seleucia, to the island of Cyprus. An island 40 miles wide and 150 miles long, Cyprus was a Roman province famous for copper mining and ship building. The island had such perfect climate and resources, it was known as Makaria—"Happy Isle." A native of Cyprus, Barnabas wanted his friends and countrymen to know Jesus. Going home, he had natural contacts. Ray Stedman commented, "As the men preached on Cyprus they obviously expected God to be with them and to open doors everywhere they went. This is the way the Holy Spirit commonly operates; we are not to wait for orders concerning everything we do. Young Christians often get the idea that they are to be like robots, automatons, ruled by computer impulses that come from the Spirit, and that they must sit and wait until such an impulse comes.

"[God] will direct us precisely at times, and when He does we must not ignore His direction. But when He doesn't we are to move out where we are with the confident expectation that God is with us and will open the doors to make a way for us. When we follow that pattern, life becomes exciting. God is infinitely creative, always doing something surprising, unexpected."[1]

During the siege of Paris in 1870, Turgenev wrote to a friend, "What a hard time we have, we who are born onlookers at life." But Christians have no business as "onlookers at life." Our place is not on the balcony but in the arena. Lacking a specific command, "Continue to work out your salvation with fear and trembling, for it is God who works in you to will and to act according to his good purpose" (Phil. 2:12-13).

To get Christians out of the "fortress mentality" is difficult at times. One frustrated pastor got impatient with the cold formality of his people sitting in their pews Sunday after Sunday, but doing nothing about their faith the remainder of

17

the week. Finally he preached a sermon on the subject, "Saints in Cellophane." He compared them with cigars neatly wrapped and arranged in a box. Unfortunately, he got fired before he got them fired up. But the New Testament makes it clear that the Christian faith must not be kept under wraps. There's no contradiction between the gathered church and the scattered church. We gather in preparation to scatter.

"When they arrived at Salamis, they proclaimed the word of God in the Jewish synagogues" (v. 5). God always had people whose hearts were open and receptive to the Good News. During their three-year missionary tour, God scheduled many divine appointments. God's Word was being planted like a seed in rich and ready soil. Like Barnabas and Saul, we are sent into divine appointments. Day after day, God provides divine appointments for us. How important that we recognize them and are quick to share God's Word.

The warmth of spirit and joy in the Sunday evening service created a hunger in Al Webb. On his way to the trailer park, he mentioned it to Myrna Tingstrom, a loyal member of my church. She faithfully traced God's plan of salvation from the letter to the Romans and pressed the claims of Jesus Christ. Al accepted the Lord as Savior. Two weeks later, Al Webb had a heart attack and went home to be with Jesus.

We are all sent at different times into divine appointments.

Like Barnabas and Saul, we are sent into a secular world. Traveling 100 miles from Salamis, they arrived in Paphos, capital city of the island. A strong, tough Roman garrison guarded the Greek culture, which was permeated with the worship of Venus, goddess of love. Venus was a byword for lustful immorality. Secular society, as today, had immersed itself in sexual excitement. Moral purity, as even now, was scoffed at by people bent on pleasure at any cost. Into that kind of world, tough and luring, God sends His people.

18

Superstition, a sign of decadence, was popular then, similar to today's rise in the occult, the bizarre, and drug abuse. Men of wealth hired private soothsayers and magicians who dealt in fortune-telling and astrology. Sergius Paulus, governor of Cyprus, had hired a private wizard, but there remained in Sergius Paulus a heart hunger. Having heard of Barnabas and Saul, he called for them to speak the Word of God.

But Elymas Bar-Jesus, a turncoat Jew and a false prophet, saw an attack on his meal ticket! "Elymas the sorcerer . . . opposed them and tried to turn the proconsul from the faith" (v. 8). Elymas attempted to turn the governor away from God's Word by twisting, distorting, and perverting truth. He would barter that man's soul for his own personal gain. The same callous, calculating, carnal world today gleefully rings its cash registers trading in pornography, alcohol, drugs, and moral filth that destroy the bodies, minds, and souls of our people. All for personal gain! Truth always sets men's minds free from the grip of superstition and the occult.

Here a new kind of opposition was introduced to Christianity. Before Acts 13, opposition had come from religious prejudice and unbelief—a denial of Jesus' resurrection. From this point on, opposition by the secular world came from motives of greed, self-seeking, prestige, and power. Elymas "opposed them," meaning "to stand against someone, face-to-face." It portrays the familiar picture of a baseball umpire and an angered coach yelling nose-to-nose!

Yet God calls us to greatness in an hour like this: "Therefore, prepare your minds for action; be self-controlled; set your hope fully on the grace to be given you when Jesus Christ is revealed. As obedient children, do not conform to the evil desires you had when you lived in ignorance. But just as he who called you is holy, so be holy in all you do" (1 Pet. 1:13-15).

Like Barnabas and Saul, we are sent to minister through our spiritual gifts. The success with which Saul confronted

Elymas confirms his spiritual gifts of apostleship and discernment of spirits. First Corinthians 12:8-10 contains a partial list of spiritual gifts. Among them it says, "distinguishing between spirits" (v. 10). Saul detected the phony, confronting him face-to-face. That is a spiritual gift. Since I don't have that gift, I accept everyone at face value. But often God has placed people gifted with discernment around me to protect me and His church.

The Bible says, "Now to each one the manifestation of the Spirit is given for the common good" (1 Cor. 12:7). After a partial listing of spiritual gifts, the Bible adds: "All these are the work of one and the same Spirit, and he gives them to each one, just as he determines" (v. 11). Paul explains, "So in Christ, we who are many form one body, and each member belongs to all the others. We have different gifts, according to the grace given us" (Rom. 12:5-6). As a believer, you are sent to minister through your spiritual gifts. If you decline to minister or neglect your gift(s), the Body of Christ suffers.

J. Oswald Sanders noted, "The placing of Saul with Barnabas was no chance happening. Barnabas was mature, experienced, a 'son of consolation.' To his gracious gifts the Holy Spirit added the intensity, the fiery zeal, the restless urgency, the brilliant intellectual powers of Saul, who had long been preparing in the school of God. Together they made a wonderful blending of gifts."[2] God blends us together, overlapping our gifts—where one is weak, another is made strong. Each one contributes to the work of God's kingdom.

When Jesus called His men, He said, "Come, follow me, . . . and I will *make* you fishers of men" (Mark 1:17, italics added). These fellows were anything but "fishers of men" when He called them. He didn't say, "Follow Me *because* you are fishers of men." But He said, "I will *make* you fishers of men."

Jesus still calls people to service. He calls people with no experience. He calls people who don't feel qualified. He says,

20

"If you *follow Me,* I will *make* you qualified workers." How are you planning to serve this year?

We Are Filled with the Holy Spirit

"Then Saul, who was also called Paul, filled with the Holy Spirit, looked straight at Elymas and said, 'You are a child of the devil and an enemy of everything that is right! You are full of all kinds of deceit and trickery. Will you never stop perverting the right ways of the Lord? Now the hand of the Lord is against you. You are going to be blind, and for a time you will be unable to see the light of the sun.' Immediately mist and darkness came over him, and he groped about, seeking someone to lead him by the hands. When the proconsul saw what had happened, he believed, for he was amazed at the teaching about the Lord" (vv. 9-12).

Faced with this tough situation, God's Spirit filled Saul, empowering him for the challenge. The occasion demanded inspiration that only God can give. Saul's supply of God's Spirit was sufficient to handle that emergency.

When God calls and sends us, we can depend on His filling. When circumstances seem insurmountable, the Spirit's filling provides God's resources. He is our great Enabler, equipping us for service.

A rookie executive went to the company president about a difficult problem in his department. The president advised, "Young man, in our company, we don't have problems. We have opportunities."

The young man pressed on, "Then, sir, I'd like to talk to you about an insurmountable opportunity!"

Fortunately, when God's Spirit calls and sends us, He equips us to deal with insurmountable opportunities! Saul won such an astounding victory in the Lord, he took a new name, Paul—a Gentile name to match his mission to the Gentile world. William P. Barker wrote, ". . . in Hebrew tradition great victories were sometimes celebrated by taking new

21

names, as when Abram became Abraham, Jacob became Israel, Simon became Peter. The change from Saul to Paul signified a victory among the Gentiles, and signalled a shift in the Spirit's activity."[3]

The Spirit's filling makes us bold. Led by the Spirit, Paul silenced the false teacher. He would not tolerate that man to stand in the way of Sergius' salvation. There comes a time to be firm. Silence is not always golden—sometimes it is yellow! In occasions demanding boldness, we need the mind of Christ—seeking to turn people's hopes to Jesus!

John Witherspoon, a clergyman and president of the College of New Jersey, was one of the signers of the Declaration of Independence. As he took up his pen to sign, Witherspoon announced, "There is a tide in the affairs of men, a nick of time. We perceive it now before us. To hesitate is to consent to our own slavery. He that will not respond is unworthy the name of a free man."

Being filled with the Spirit gives courage to do the right in the face of opposition. Paul demonstrated that Jesus Christ is more powerful than any of man's devising. As a result, the governor of Cyprus' spiritual adviser was left groping for someone to lead him by the hand. Perhaps there's an element of mercy in Elymas' sudden blindness. Paul may have remembered how his own sudden blindness had turned him to Jesus Christ and brought light to his life.

The Spirit's filling empowers spiritual success. "When the proconsul saw what had happened, he believed, for he was amazed at the teaching about the Lord" (v. 12). This was Paul's first presentation of Christ to a Roman official. God's Spirit brought victory, resulting in the conversion of Sergius Paulus, one of the curators of the banks of the Tiber during the reign of Claudius. A Latin inscription to him remains today. Without the Spirit's filling, the opportunity would have ended in disaster. It makes a difference if our service is *"for* the Lord" or *"of* the Lord!"

22

Unaware of the Spirit's filling, we tend to look for specialists or professionals when opportunity comes. But God wishes to empower *you* and give *you* spiritual success. Jerry Cook gave this beautiful illustration:

A phone call came one day from a woman who had been a Christian for only two or three weeks. She said, "I've been talking to my neighbor and she wants to receive Christ. Could you come and talk to her?"

I said sure, walked out and got in my car and started down the road. I had gone no more than 5 or 6 blocks when the Lord began to speak to me. I knew in a flash what He was saying: "If you go there I will honor My Word and on the basis of her trust in Me that woman will be saved, but I will hold you responsible for stealing the reward of one of My sheep."

I said, "I don't understand that. She is going to get saved and I am going to be judged?" It didn't make sense. Nevertheless, the Lord's word to me was so strong and so definite that I knew I couldn't go. I turned around and went back to my office. On the way back I got a short but intensive course in pastor-people relations. I remembered a deep-sea fishing trip my wife Barbara and I had taken recently. She had tied into a shark out there—a big dude about 8 feet long. She was having a ball trying to play out that shark. About that time one of the crew members came, took her pole from her and landed the shark for her. What a letdown. He had taken away her victory, and she resented it.

The Lord said, "Jerry, that's exactly what you've been doing as a pastor. You have been running in, taking away the ministry of the people, thinking you're doing them a favor. But I'm going to judge you for stealing their rewards." It was heavy.

I called the woman on the phone and told her I couldn't come, and I told her why.

She said, "But I don't know what to do. I don't know what to say."

I said, "Do you know Jesus?"

"Well, yes."

"If you know someone, you can introduce that person to anyone, can't you? What happened when you were introduced to Jesus? Were any Scriptures used? You could use those same verses if you want to. But just introduce your neighbor to Jesus the same way you were introduced to Him. If it worked for you it will work for her."

She agreed to try it, and we had prayer together on the phone. Less than an hour later, there came a knock on my study door. Here stood this woman and her neighbor, both glowing as if they had strobe lights on their faces. Not only had the neighbor been gloriously saved, but both women had begun to understand that leading people to Christ is not the exclusive work of a few well-trained professionals. Any Christian can do it.[4]

When the Holy Spirit fills, He will use you with great success. He handpicked you for greatness!

The Spirit's filling enables self-acceptance. Self-acceptance is probably one of the great battlefields. The call to greatness can be hindered by a lack of self-acceptance. Someone suggested an addition to the Beatitudes: "Blessed are they who give us back our self-respect." Jesus came to do that! Everywhere He went He restored people's self-respect. And by the Spirit's filling He would restore your self-respect.

Saul had persecuted the church, consented to Stephen's death, and jailed Christians. Upon his conversion, he desired to be an apostle to the Jews—but failed in Damascus, tried again in Jerusalem, and was sent home to Tarsus for several years while the church returned to a state of peace and order. Saul was plagued with self-despisings, but one day Barnabas

24

showed up in Tarsus and coaxed Saul to come with him to Antioch where they worked together in the church for a year.

Now, in God's timing, watch the changing roles: "Barnabas and Saul" (Acts 12:25); "Barnabas, Simeon . . . Lucius . . . Manaen . . . and Saul" (13:1); "Barnabas and Saul" (v. 2); "Barnabas and Saul" (v. 7); "Then Saul . . . called Paul" (v. 9); "Paul and his companions" (v. 13). After Acts 13:13 it was always "Paul and Barnabas." Barnabas had been the leader of this missionary team, but now the roles reversed: Paul and Barnabas.

Two beautiful things stand out here. First, Barnabas made the transition without struggle. Though Barnabas had seniority, Saul had superior gifts of leadership. Barnabas switched to second fiddle without missing a beat. The important thing to him was to see God's work prosper and move forward. Although the adjustment was probably difficult, he had no room for smallness. Barnabas was called to greatness.

Bernard Newman stayed in a Bulgarian peasant's home. All during his visit the peasant's daughter was stitching away on a dress. Newman asked, "Don't you ever get tired of that eternal sewing?"

"Oh, no," she responded. "This is my wedding dress; it's a labor of love!"

Barnabas would take any assignment for Jesus Christ. It was always a labor of love.

Second, Paul willingly accepted the leadership role. He didn't shrink back or seek a less demanding assignment. Whatever God had assigned, Paul was on call. When your selfhood is secure in the Lord, you can accept changing roles without exalting or diminishing yourself. It is all of God. God calls, sends, and fills us with His Holy Spirit. He handpicked us for greatness!

An executive of the Gruen Watch Company said, "I have never met a lazy man. I have only met unchallenged men. Challenge releases energy into a man. Challenge creates energy and gives direction. Challenge makes a man willing to pay the price of discipline. A football coach does not get many young men to cut out excess sweets and dates, to go to bed early, and to sweat out practice without the dream of getting on the squad. . . . That's what is wrong with the Christian life as we often present it today. We offer no challenge. We just tell people to stop enjoying themselves, join the church, and be miserable. We ask them to stay in rigorous training, but we don't get them in the game. We may have a huddle coming up or a meeting of the team, but no real, face-to-face, toe-to-toe encounter!"

Let's think big of our labors of love. Let's accept His challenge of service for Jesus' sake. We who represent Jesus are called to greatness.

2

Betting Your Life
on God

Acts 13:13-52

The caption in big black letters said: "SHE HAD 'GOOD LIFE' BUT SHE CHOSE TO DIE." *Los Angeles Times* staff writer Patt Morrison explained vividly:

> When the farewell letters were written, when the draft of her will was folded and left under the telephone in her bedroom, Rosemary Russell locked up her Dover Shores home in Newport Beach, got into her Mercedes . . . and drove away to die.

> The life that Rose Russell chose to leave was a life many people would have envied.

> At 25, it seemed that life had already given her a generous portion, with her California good looks and the bright ambition that had prompted her to apply to law school.

> On top of that, Russell was more successful at 25 than many men at 50. Her annual income had grown to $75,000 in 2 years. She was a partner with her brother in a real estate and investment firm and she owned a staggering string of properties—including her own home and the silver Mercedes, with its "BELLY UP" license plates a taunting, laughing dare at the bankruptcy she never had to worry about.

But there are other kinds of bankruptcy. Russell had family and friends who loved her, but it evidently was not enough.

Because last week—after a 6-year romance broke up—Russell, a meticulous, deliberate young woman who could figure out fine-print escrow clauses, set out just as meticulously and deliberately to end a life in which, she wrote, she was "so tired of clapping with one hand."

The article gave more details but ended with a letter she sent to a pair of friends: "Just do me a favor, so it won't all be for nothing. Don't let the pursuit of money and success interfere in the beautiful relationship you two have. As long as you have each other, and a strong faith in God, you'll want for nothing else."

Apparently that beautiful young lady had bet her life on wealth, things, achievement, and whimsical feelings of human love. It was not enough! Perhaps she had seen a glimmer of hope in the couple to whom she had written that letter: "As long as you have each other, and a strong faith in God, you'll want for nothing else!" For some unknown reason, she did not know how to reach out for God.

Ultimately, everyone puts his trust in someone or something. At some point, everyone makes some kind of leap of faith. The Bible calls us to bet our lives on God.

If you have everything you could possibly want, you know by now it doesn't satisfy. If you have absolutely nothing, you have nothing to lose. Put your trust in God, and you can make life count. Bet your life on God! You can depend on Him.

Paul and Barnabas did. They left the island of Cyprus, Barnabas' birthplace, sailing about 120 miles to Asia Minor where Paul had been born. Leaving the ship at Perga, the travelers found a hot, steamy, mosquito-ridden malarial hole.

28

Apparently Paul contracted malaria and was left physically weak.

John Mark had had enough. He headed back for Jerusalem while Paul and Barnabas followed the population shift into the highlands. On the rugged, 100-mile journey, they forded two of the most treacherous rivers in the world and went into the Taurus mountains, which were infested with robbers terrorizing caravans. Paul never forgot that tour. He referred to it in a letter: "I have been in danger from rivers, in danger from bandits, in danger from my own countrymen, in danger from Gentiles; . . . I have labored and toiled and have often gone without sleep; I have known hunger and thirst and have often gone without food" (2 Cor. 11:26-27).

Paul and his group finally arrived in Antioch near Pisidia, one of the towns of Galatia that Greek colonists had founded under Roman control. On the Sabbath, Paul and Barnabas attended the local synagogue. After prayers and reading of the Law and Prophets, the man in charge turned to the visitors: "Brothers, if you have a message of encouragement for the people, please speak" (v. 15).

Without hesitation, Paul stood up to speak—a Greek custom of oratory unlike the Jewish custom of sitting to teach. Acts 13 contains Paul's first recorded sermon. With the Spirit's anointing, Paul called the people to bet their lives on God! Times have changed, but human need and God's love have not!

Bet Your Life on the Announcement of God's Grace

In verses 17-37, Paul traced the biblical history of God's guidance and grace. He declared that God has brought about His purposes in time and space.

Paul's sermon is reminiscent of Stephen's address and Peter's preaching, but introduces his own emphasis of being justified by faith—betting your life on God! Making a quick historical survey, Paul believed God is at work. God's history is not a haphazard, tangled ball of thread. Meaning and moral law are at work in the universe. God is in control, and He is working out His purposes. As Maltbie Babcock put it:

> This is my Father's world,
> Oh, let me ne'er forget
> That though the wrong
> Seems oft so strong,
> God is the Ruler yet.

The story of God's grace told of the deliverance of God's people (v. 17), of God's patience with them (v. 18), of God's care (v. 19). In fact, Paul listed 11 different instances of God's work in history. God's grace working through the whole Bible culminated in the coming of Jesus. Many people think of the Bible as a collection of disconnected stories strung together—and miss the essential message.

On December 17, 1903, Orville and Wilbur Wright succeeded in getting their funny-looking machine up in the air for 59 seconds. Elated at their success, they sent a telegram back to their sister in Dayton, Ohio: "First sustained flight today 59 seconds. Hope to be home by Christmas."

Excited about the news, the sister took the telegram to the editor of the local newspaper. The headlines in the paper the next morning said: "POPULAR LOCAL BICYCLE MERCHANTS TO BE HOME FOR HOLIDAYS." As Charles Hembree said, "The scoop of the century was missed because the editor missed the point. We laugh when we read this account, but many times we have missed the point of some scriptures because we have read them too casually and not let their deep meaning sink into our souls."[1]

God's promises of a Savior were fulfilled in the ministry, crucifixion, and resurrection of Jesus Christ. Someone said, "Love letters are the campaign promises of the heart." The Bible is God's love letter to you and me. You can depend on His promises! Bet your life on what the Bible says. Take it to heart and take it seriously.

A pastor called in the home of a sick parishioner. Wishing to read a few verses of encouragement, he asked for the family's Bible. The sick woman called to her little girl in the next room with a syrupy voice: "Dear, would you get that old book your mother loves so well?" Promptly the little girl walked in with the Sears catalog!

Above all, treasure the Bible's announcement of God's great grace. Bet your life that it is dependable.

Bet Your Life on the Application of God's Grace

After tracing God's work in history and the fulfillment of His promise in Jesus, Paul said: "Therefore, my brothers, I want you to know that through Jesus the forgiveness of sins is proclaimed to you. Through him everyone who believes is justified from everything you could not be justified from by the law of Moses" (vv. 38-39). Having told of God's grace, Paul jumped right into the question: "So what?" God's mercy and love are given for you. You can personally know and experience God's love! Bet your life on it!

A skeptical man sat down to read the Bible one hour every evening. After a while he said to his wife, "If this Book is right, we are wrong." A few evenings later he remarked, "If this Book is right, we are lost." One night he rejoiced, "If this Book is right, we can be saved!" And they were.

Paul spoke of the proclamation of forgiveness: "through Jesus the forgiveness of sins is proclaimed to you" (v. 38). That's Good News! The Bible tells us: "For all have sinned and fall short of the glory of God, and are justified freely by his grace through the redemption that came by Christ Jesus" (Rom. 3:23-24). That means there is no saint without a past—but no sinner without a future! Yes, "The wages of sin is death, but the gift of God is eternal life in Christ Jesus our Lord" (Rom. 6:23).

Paul spoke of the power of forgiveness: "Through him everyone who believes is justified from everything you could not be justified from by the law" (v. 39). In later years, Paul wrote back to the Christians in Pisidian Antioch: "A man is not justified by observing the law, but by faith in Jesus Christ. So we, too, have put our faith in Christ Jesus that we may be justified by faith in Christ and not by observing the law, because by observing the law no one will be justified" (Gal. 2:16). Forgiveness comes from God's willingness to treat us as if we had not sinned. In biblical terminology this is called "justification" or "being justified by God." As a result, we are made "righteous," meaning "put into a right relationship with God." God's forgiveness has the power to change us—to make us new creations in His sight. His forgiveness produces a change in us that "being good" could not.

The Law was directed to people of a fallen creation. God's grace makes people new creations. The Law revealed what was in man—sin and rebellion; grace reveals what is in God—unmerited love. The Law demands man to be righteous; grace brings man into a right relationship. The Law speaks of what man must do for God; grace tells what God has done for man. The Law gives a knowledge of sin; grace removes sin.

Paul spoke of the possibility of forgiveness. Forgiveness can be our personal possession. Jesus is God's provision for our forgiveness, but there's a difference between His provision and our possession. Faith takes God's provision as our possession.

God's forgiveness is not a theory but a love affair. God's grace is never some impersonal doctrine, but His free gift of eternal life, of abundant life here and now, the offer of a guilt-free life. Betting your life on God is the only way to receive God's gift—by faith alone! God's forgiveness is just a prayer away! Applying God's grace is a personal act of faith.

In 1830, George Wilson was condemned to die for robbing the United States Mail. Less than eight hours before his midnight deadline, the president of the United States, Andrew

Jackson, granted him an official pardon. Signed papers were taken to the federal prison.

When George Wilson received the pardon embossed with the presidential seal, the cell was unlocked. Strangely, George Wilson refused the president's forgiveness, walked to the gallows, and was executed with a pardon in his pocket.

Why? Because he refused to acknowledge his guilt. By refusing to admit his guilt, he rejected his only means of life. Legally, a pardon is an act of grace that must be accepted before it is valid.

Some people refuse to admit they are sinners. And God's available pardon and gift of life are ignored or rejected. God has provided His Son Jesus as the sacrificial pardon. God has delivered His pardon, but it is not complete without your acceptance. What better offers do you have? I urge you to bet your life on the Lord!

Bet Your Life on the Adequacy of God's Grace

After Paul's sermon, the congregation was dismissed, but many crowded around to hear more. People invited them to come back on the next Sabbath to speak again. "Paul and Barnabas . . . talked with them and urged them to continue in the grace of God" (v. 43). God's grace can keep and protect His children. No wonder Paul "urged them to continue in the grace of God."

God's grace keeps those who have bet their lives on God. The Bible says, "They were very glad and rejoiced in Paul's message; and as many as wanted eternal life, believed" (v. 48, TLB).

Christian psychologist Clyde Narramore declares, "If you are a believer, your sins are forgiven! It makes no difference whether you *feel* it or not—it does not change the facts. You may *think* your sins are not forgiven, but God says they *are* forgiven. So they are.

33

"... A lady from the Midwest wrote me a letter saying that although she was born-again and daily asked forgiveness of sin, a wrong she had done many years ago was still tormenting her. I wrote this dear lady, ... (suggesting) that she read the 51st Psalm several times. Then I pointed out that no matter what she *thought* about her past sins, she couldn't possibly change the fact that they *were* forgiven.

"'It's your feelings over against God's Word,' I added. 'Wouldn't you prefer to believe God?'

"When the lady really believed God, she soon had victory ... and ceased her doubting."[2]

God's grace keeps those who are being tested and tried. Betting their lives on God and believing in Jesus Christ, "The word of the Lord spread through the whole region" (v. 49). Any time men and women come to God, don't be surprised at persecution in one form or another. Sure enough, "They stirred up persecution against Paul and Barnabas, and expelled them from their region" (v. 50). The devil doesn't like it when you begin trusting God. He bids high for your soul, but God's only begotten Son Jesus has paid it all at the Cross. Satan is a defeated enemy. God's grace will keep you and hold you through every test and trial.

Persecution broke out that dogged Paul's tracks for the remainder of his life. Later, from his final prison, Paul wrote his last known letter to a young pastor, Timothy. In that farewell address, Paul said, "For God did not give us a spirit of timidity, but a spirit of power, of love and of self-discipline. ... This grace was given us in Christ Jesus before the beginning of time, but it has now been revealed through the appearing of our Savior, Christ Jesus, who has destroyed death and has brought life and immortality to light through the gospel. ... I am not ashamed, because I know whom I have believed, and am convinced that he is able to guard what I have entrusted to him for that day" (2 Tim. 1:7, 9-10, 12).

34

My God has promised to keep you through every storm in life. His grace is adequate.

A gray-haired lady rode on a rough flight out of Kansas City. That great airplane dropped and regained altitude like a confused elevator. Nearly all the passengers were sick or frightened. But she sat calmly. The person next to her commented, "I'm surprised you don't get airsick."

She smiled and replied, "I have a preventive for airsickness this morning."

"For goodness' sake, what is it?" asked the passenger. "Tell me so I can try it."

Confidently the lady said, "I keep my eyes on the sunrise."

When all of life seems to have lost its bearings, bet your life on God. There's a sunrise of joy coming your way that you'll never get over. Keep your eyes on the sunrise—Jesus Christ. He is our Sun of Righteousness who arises with healing in His wings! "For I am convinced that neither death nor life, neither angels nor demons, neither the present nor the future, nor any powers, neither height nor depth, nor anything else in all creation, will be able to separate us from the love of God that is in Christ Jesus our Lord" (Rom. 8:38-39).

Martin Luther, surviving many trials for his faith in God, wrote: "Faith is a living, daring confidence in God's grace. It is so sure and certain that a man could stake his life on it a thousand times!" If you bet your life on the adequacy of God's grace, I cannot guarantee that the stars will shine brighter tonight or that when you wake tomorrow a new world will open before you. But I do guarantee, on the authority of God's Word, that Jesus will keep that which you have committed to Him. He keeps His every promise.

Tests and trials may come—but you can face them like the nine-year-old girl who left a note for her father: "Dear Dad, I am up at school jumping hurdles. Love, Karen." I like that spirit: "I am jumping hurdles!" God's grace can make us overcomers: "In all these things we are more than conquerors through him who loved us" (Rom. 8:37).

Senator Harold Hughes came home one cold January night in Iowa. His house was as dark and empty as his soul. His wife, Eva, had taken their children and left. They could no longer stand his horrible alcoholic addiction.

Hopelessly Senator Hughes called all through the house. No answer came but the hollow echo of his own voice. He had tried everything to quit drinking, but couldn't. Slumped onto his bed, sunk in despair, he looked for a way to escape his horrible self-loathing. He thought to himself, Why go on doing the things I hate? He realized, The more I thought about the disorder in my life and the inability to control it, the more I wanted to end it. I was just an evil, rotten drunk, a liar. I deserved to die!

His hungry heart felt no satisfaction. Life had lost its meaning. Senator Hughes went to the bathroom and prepared to take his own life with a shotgun. Suddenly he began talking to God, trying to explain his tragic plan. Kneeling down on the cold tiles of the floor, he began to sense God dealing with him.

In his own words, he described it: "In the quiet bathroom, a strange peace gently settled over me. Something that I had never experienced before was happening, something far beyond my senseless struggles. A warm peace seemed to settle deep within me, filling the terrible emptiness, driving out the self-hate and condemnation. My sins seemed to evaporate like moisture spots under a hot, bright sun.

"God was reaching down and touching me. A God who cared, who loved me, who was concerned for me despite my sins. Like a stricken child lost in a storm, I had suddenly stumbled into the warm arms of my Father. Joy filled me, so intense it seemed to burst my breast.

"Kneeling on that bathroom floor, I gave myself to Him totally."

36

Putting away his shotgun, Senator Hughes felt a chilling doubt. Was this just another illusion—like so many others he'd had? But in that moment of doubt, he sensed something stronger than doubt saying, "Stay with God. Follow Him. Believe!"

Kneeling beside his bed he prayed, "Father, I don't understand this or know why I deserve it. You know how weak I am. But I put myself in Your hands. Please give my family back to me—and give me strength never to run again. Father, I put myself in Your hands."

God brought that family back together again in a beautiful way. Senator Hughes has become a well-known, outstanding example of God's grace. As a faithful Christian, Harold Hughes was instrumental in leading Charles Colson and other national figures to Jesus.

Years passed by. When a third daughter, Phyllis, was about seven years old, she asked, rather surprised, about his past drinking problem. Tears of gratitude filled his eyes, and he hugged his little girl: "Honey, I did drink once. Much of it happened before you were born. I stopped drinking before you were old enough to remember. Yes, Honey, your daddy did have a very sad drinking problem."

Putting her arms around his big neck, she responded, "But you don't drink now—and that's all that matters."

What we are doing today through Jesus is all that matters to God! Will you bet your life on God?

3

What Is Our Mission?

Acts 14

It's important to know what you're trying to do before you can know if you are succeeding or failing.

Acts 14 describes the second half of Paul and Barnabas' 1,400 mile missionary journey. Their tour may have taken from two to four years. Luke tells how they came back to Antioch, their starting point, for a time of rest, recuperation, replenishment, recruitment, reorganization for a second trip, and a report of their progress: "On arriving there, they gathered the church together and reported all that God had done through them and how he had opened the door of faith to the Gentiles" (v. 27).

Reading through Acts 14, one discovers Paul and Barnabas caused riots in two out of three cities where they lingered to preach. Nothing stirs up the devil like success! Though Paul was run out of Iconium, he took the opportunity to preach. After all, a leader is one who, when being run out of town, makes it look like he's leading a parade! In Lystra, Paul was stoned and dragged half-dead out of the city. It made quite an indelible impression on Paul, for he wrote years later, "once I was stoned" (2 Cor. 11:25). Writing back to these same south Galatian churches, he said, "I bear on my body the marks of Jesus" (Gal. 6:17).

From our perspective, Paul's first missionary journey seems disastrous—or, at least, less than wonderful. However, the tour must be interpreted in the light of its mission. The reason for going affects what one accomplishes.

A certain shoe company sent a salesman into the Appalachian hill country of eastern Tennessee. After a time, he came back discouraged and with little success. His reason for failure was simply, "They don't wear shoes!" Another salesman was assigned the same territory. He came back excited and enthused, having sold all his shoes. The reason for his success, he exclaimed, "They didn't have any shoes!"

The church must know its mission before it can know if it is succeeding or failing!

A pastor, speaking to a group of college students, asked the leader of the fraternity house, "What are you living for?"

The student leader replied, "I am going to be a pharmacist."

The pastor pressed further: "That's how you are going to earn your money—but what are you living for?"

After a moment's thought, the young man answered honestly with bewilderment, "Sir, I am sorry—but I haven't thought that through yet!"

Asking the group the same question, the minister found that only 2 out of the 30 students had seriously faced the issue: "What is my reason for living?"

What is your reason for living? And what is our mission as a church?

I have been working on a statement to embody the mission of the church. It may not be complete, but I have begun with this statement: "Our purpose is to make disciples of Jesus in the power of the Holy Spirit and to exercise God-given spiritual gifts for building up the Body of Christ."

We must know where we are headed to know if we're succeeding or not. Many churches assume they know their mission but are like the airline pilot who announced, "Ladies and gentlemen, I have some good news and bad news. The bad news is that we are lost. The good news is that we are making excellent time!"

The unswerving loyalty of Paul and Barnabas in Acts 14 to their God-called mission encourages us to know and follow our mission.

Like Paul and Barnabas, Our Mission Includes a Ministry of Grace

"At Iconium Paul and Barnabas . . . spoke so effectively that a great number of Jews and Gentiles believed. . . . So Paul and Barnabas spent considerable time there, speaking boldly for the Lord, who confirmed the message of his grace by enabling them to do miraculous signs and wonders" (vv. 1, 3).

People were getting saved. Labeled "apostles" for the first time (v. 4), Paul and Barnabas preached and testified to the saving grace of God. Many turned to the Lord Jesus Christ. When opposition flared, the missionaries decided to stay longer. The message of grace flourished in the hearts of the people.

"The message of his grace" (v. 3) was not a rehearsal of their own ideas nor did it have the dull ring, "This is what I think" or "This is where I am coming from." The word of grace told what God had already accomplished through Jesus Christ. The Good News speaks of Jesus' life, death, and resurrection, and the promise of His abiding Spirit. Grace is not a salvation we earn. It is a salvation already earned by Jesus' completed work—grace: "God's Riches At Christ's Expense!"

This message of grace includes the promise of God's great enablement through the Holy Spirit.

Thomas Carlyle, sitting by his old mother in front of the fireplace, complained against the preachers in his day: "If I had to preach, I would go into the pulpit and say no more than this: 'All you people know what you ought to do. Well, go and do it.'"

40

His mother continued knitting in silence. Soon she replied, "Aye, my boy; and will ye tell them how?"

Man needs redeeming grace to be lifted to new levels of Christian character. Only God's grace enables spiritual recovery. Our mission today is a ministry of grace. With fervency, we must give ourselves to the mission—to make disciples in the power of the Spirit. That involves more than scattering seeds of testimony. It includes intercessory prayer, personal involvement, and pressing the claims of Christ. People should be getting saved! Making disciples means more than changing peoples' thoughts or creeds—it is bringing about spiritual revolution. It is guiding them to confession of Christ, to acceptance of God's forgiveness, and to taking hold of new life in Christ.

C. S. Lewis wrote, "No clever arrangement of bad eggs ever made a good omelet." Only Jesus' miracle of transformation of life meets our deep need.

The Barbers' Supply Association held a convention in a large hotel. An enthusiastic publicity agent went to skid row and picked up the most unpromising derelict. Unkempt, unshaven, drunken, down-and-out, he was taken to the hotel. The barbers gave him a haircut, dressed him up in a new suit, and bought him a stylish overcoat with all the extras of fashion. They put him up in a nice room. When introduced at the convention, he looked like an ideal of the barber's art. The daily newspaper had photographed and publicized each step of the transformation. Everyone was amazed at how handsomely he could be made over.

Extremely impressed, the hotel manager told the man, "You're quite a gentleman now! I'm going to give you a great opportunity at a job in my hotel. I'll back you. We are going to make a successful man out of you!"

The next morning his eight o'clock appointment was broken. The hotel manager finally found him back on skid row dead drunk, sleeping on newspapers in an alley, his fashionable clothes wrinkled and dirty. The manager spoke of his disillusionment: "The barbers may be able to clean him up on the outside, but you can never make anything out of a man until you change him on the inside."

And that's exactly what Jesus came to do. Our mission is to speak the word of grace—and people will be getting saved! Let's give ourselves to spreading the good news of Jesus and introducing people to Him. He alone brings about transformation of the heart. The Church is not a company on a summer porch; it is a life-saving crew.

Like Paul and Barnabas, Our Mission Includes a Ministry of Wholeness

"In Lystra there sat a man crippled in his feet, who was lame from birth and had never walked. He listened to Paul as he was speaking. Paul looked directly at him, saw that he had faith to be healed and called out, 'Stand up on your feet!' At that, the man jumped up and began to walk" (vv. 8-10).

People were being healed and made whole. The city of Lystra had no synagogue, so the missionaries went to the marketplace—always buzzing with people. Beggars, often lame and deformed, hung around, hopeless and broken. People usually ignored them, considering them cursed by the gods of fate. There sat a man "crippled in his feet" (v. 8). That word "crippled" or "impotent" (KJV) regularly means "impossible." From a human point of view his case was impossible—hopeless, indeed.

As Paul spoke of Jesus, hope was kindled. "Paul . . . saw that he had faith to be healed" (v. 9). Seneca once taught, "It is part of the cure to wish to be cured." "Paul . . . called out, 'Stand up on your feet!'" (v. 10). He was "asking the impossible. But when the man *willed* to obey, God furnished the power. . . . faith was demonstrated in obedience and rewarded with divine power."[1]

42

"At that, the man jumped up and began to walk" (v. 10). Notice the two verbs, "jumped up" and "began to walk," are in different grammatical tenses. He "jumped up"—he leaped with a single bound! It's the natural, joyful response at the moment of discovery—God had made him whole! God had touched him and he knew it!

The man "began to walk"—he continued walking—using the imperfect tense, which means that though he jumped up immediately, he went on walking. The grammar suggests the permanence of his cure. God's touch of wholeness is more than an emotional spurt or passing ecstasy. His touch of wholeness brings a continued relationship with the Lord, a sustained walk with Jesus. Uncle Buddy Robinson used to say, "I don't mind how high a fellow jumps, just so he walks straight when he comes back down."

Our mission is to "make disciples in the power of the Holy Spirit." A crisis experience is followed by a holy walk, cleansed and filled, indwelt and empowered by the Holy Spirit. His abiding presence brings wholeness. People should be receiving the Spirit's touch of wholeness.

A cartoon I enjoy shows two cowboys pointing to a third sitting on a table with an arrow sticking out of his chest. One cowboy calls to another one out of the picture, "Hey, Tex, come and settle an argument. Is this arrow Apache or Sioux?"

How shockingly like the church without vision. People within reach, hurting and wounded, pierced by broken homes and personal failures, while too often the church debates incidentals. I pray that God will give today's church a healing ministry. Don't you long to see God's touch of wholeness go deeper than mere physical problems? If He brings spiritual wholeness to your life, you'll be eager to see His ministry of wholeness extended!

Jerry Cook told this moving story:

> A young woman named Jackie, a fairly new Christian, walked into a major discount store in Portland.

As she passed through the prescription area she noticed a woman leaning on the counter, obviously very sick. Jackie felt an impulse to stop and pray with the woman, but she did what 90 percent of us would do and said to herself, "No, she would think I'm nuts."

Jackie did her shopping and on the way out passed the prescription counter again. The woman was now seated in a chair, still obviously very ill. And again Jackie was impressed, "Go, talk to her, pray with her." Jackie started on out the door, but she just couldn't go. So she resigned herself to become [a] . . . fool for Jesus. She went over, sat down beside the sick woman, took her by the hand and said, "I can see that you're quite sick and I don't want you to think I'm imposing, but I'm a Christian. Would you mind if I prayed for you?"

The woman began to weep. She said, "I've been sick for so long."

Jackie just held her hand and with eyes open said, "Lord Jesus, I know You love this lady, and I know You don't want her to be sick. Just because You love her, heal her and show her how much You care." That was it. They exchanged phone numbers and Jackie went home.

The next day Jackie got a phone call from this woman asking her to come to the woman's house. Jackie went. The woman's husband had stayed home from work in order to meet Jackie. The prescription the woman got the day before was unopened on the kitchen table. The woman and her husband were both . . . weeping.

The woman said, "When I came home I went to bed and slept all night. . . . I haven't slept all night for years." With her particular sickness she slept only for short periods and had to get up to take medication. Her husband thought she had died. He came in and awakened her to ask if she was OK. She said that she felt great.

He said, ". . . you haven't taken your medicine."

She said, "I know it, but I slept all night!" She then told her husband what happened at the shopping center. So he wanted to meet Jackie. The people knew practically nothing about the gospel. Jackie explained to them the love of Jesus, how they could be free from their sin, how Jesus wants people well not only physically, but on the inside. They both trusted in Jesus Christ.[2]

God wants to give us a ministry of wholeness—in the power of the Holy Spirit. As Jess Moody said, "Too many people want their church to be a quiet, comfortable operation, where nobody gets hurt and nobody gets healed!"

Let Jesus challenge us to a ministry of wholeness. For that to happen, we must guarantee three things. First, we must love people under every circumstance without exception. Second, we must accept them without reservations. Third, we must offer unreserved forgiveness no matter how miserably they fail or sin. "If people are not guaranteed these three things, they will never allow us the . . . privilege of bringing wholeness to them through the fellowship of the church."[3]

Like Paul and Barnabas, Our Mission Includes a Ministry of Encouragement

Paul and Barnabas went on to Derbe and "preached the good news in that city and won a large number of disciples. Then they returned to Lystra, Iconium and Antioch, strengthening the disciples and encouraging them to remain true to the faith. 'We must go through many hardships to enter the kingdom of God,' they said. Paul and Barnabas appointed elders for them in each church and, with prayer and fasting, committed them to the Lord, in whom they had put their trust" (vv. 21-23).

Derbe was the only city on this first missionary journey where Paul and Barnabas did not provoke a riot. Unhindered, they preached the good news of Jesus and made many disciples. After success in Derbe, the two apostles retraced their steps through all the hostile towns "strengthening the disciples and encouraging them to remain true to the faith" (v. 22). People were getting established. Paul and Barnabas' ministry of establishing the believers had four phases.

First, they brought comfort. They urged believers to "remain true," to be "fixed and settled" in the Lord. "Strengthening the disciples" means to make more firm, to give additional strength. They gave the word of encouragement.

Someone said of Edmund Burke, British statesman, "If you stood in a doorway to escape a passing shower with Edmund Burke, you would leave that doorway with your shoulders back and your head up and your heart uplifted to face the realities of life."[4]

Doubtless, the word of encouragement to the believers living amid hostility, sprang from the Scriptures Paul and Barnabas had memorized and digested into their own lives. These new Christians faced many temptations to drop out. Then, as now, some people lost their old friends or jobs. Sometimes families turned against them. Tragically, sometimes they were not quickly accepted and assimilated into the Christian community. The ministry of encouragement is desperately needed.

Second, Paul and Barnabas brought warning. They said, "We must go through many hardships to enter the kingdom of God" (v. 22). These "many hardships" suggest not the frequency of hardships, but the variety of testings—they come at you from all different directions and kinds.

The Greek word for "hardships" means literally "pressures." All Christians must face and endure pressures. As Dr. W. T. Purkiser put it, "Untested faith is an unsure faith. Faith grows strong and steady only as it is exercised against the hard pressures of adverse circumstances."[5] Under the pressures, have faith in God.

Third, Paul and Barnabas gave organization. They "appointed elders for them in each church" (v. 23), who probably performed the same scope of leadership exercised by "elders" in Jewish synagogues. Since synagogues no longer welcomed the apostles, they had to organize independently. Organization is not only necessary but also inevitable. Wherever human beings gather, some form of organization takes place—formal or informal. The informal can be as powerful as the formal. The Holy Spirit can transform organization into something that encourages personal growth.

Fourth, Paul and Barnabas trusted God to keep them. They "committed them to the Lord in whom they had put their trust" (v. 23). The word "committed," a Greek banking term, means to trust one's valuables or money to the safekeeping of a bank. Paul and Barnabas deposited their new converts with the Lord for safekeeping. Later Paul testified, "For I . . . am persuaded that he is able to keep that which I have committed unto him against that day" (2 Tim. 1:12, KJV).

Our mission is "to make disciples of Jesus in the power of the Holy Spirit and to exercise God-given spiritual gifts for building up the Body of Christ." If we obey the Holy Spirit, the Body of Christ will be built up and established. God has promised!

Our mission must include the ministry of encouragement.

In Baseball's Hall of Fame, Babe Ruth's glove, bat, and locker are on display. Along with the mementos is a painting of a little league player. The boy with baseball cap and bat is looking eagerly toward the pitcher's mound. He already has two strikes against him. However, behind him the artist has painted the figure of Babe Ruth. The caption below reads, "Come on, kid. You can make it!"

Christian, if you'll look over your shoulder of discouragement, you will find Jesus standing by, saying, "Come on, My child. You can make it!"

On the Isle of Patmos, the aged apostle John saw Jesus: "Then he placed his right hand on me and said: 'Do not be afraid. I am the First and the Last. I am the Living One; I was dead, and behold I am alive for ever and ever! And I hold the keys of death and Hades'" (Rev. 1:17-18).

At the journey's end, Paul and Barnabas could report, "Mission accomplished!" We, too, must continue a ministry of grace, a ministry of wholeness, and a ministry of encouragement if we are to "make disciples of Jesus in the power of the Holy Spirit and to exercise God-given spiritual gifts for building up the Body of Christ."

When Dr. Charles Strickland was district superintendent down in Florida during World War II, one little church was headed for bankruptcy because money was so scarce. They owed $15,000. Dr. Strickland had been called in to preach the last sermon in that little church before closing the doors and turning it over to the bank. He had a difficult time coming up with a theme for a church closing.

The day came. With sad heart, he went to preach the last sermon because no one had come up with the past-due $15,000. During the service, however, the Lord really helped him. Since the wartime speeches of Winston Churchill had inspired many and lingered in their memories, Dr. Strickland got enthused and began waxing eloquent about "fighting on the beaches, in the streets, and in the alleys . . ."

At the conclusion of his message, an old man stood up in the audience. He was poorly dressed, but he walked toward the altar of the church. With tears and quavering voice, he said, "I built this building with my own hands. My children were dedicated and raised here in this little church building. My sweet wife was buried from here. I just don't want to keep on living without my little church. Here's my savings-account book. It's not much, but it's all I've got."

After a moment of silence, someone else came forward and placed the contents of a purse on the altar. One after another they came forward until all were at the front of that little church.

When Dr. Strickland gathered up everything placed on the altar there was more than $16,000 worth of negotiable items. You can't imagine the joy of those who had given their all—nor the surprise of the banker the next morning!

The people had been concerned and had prayed for their little church. The future seemed impossible and bleak, so they prayed and sacrificed.

Dr. Strickland noticed that two ladies had been missing from the church service. He found out that they had been praying in a back room since dawn—and all during the morning service. They told Dr. Strickland, "Oh, we prayed through on our little church early this morning, so we've been praying for you, Brother Strickland. About the time we thought you were minding God, we started to come into the church service—but then you started talking about 'fighting in the streets and alleys,' so we went back to praying. God has heard our prayers!"

Today that church is prosperous and could raise $15,000 in five minutes. It has had a mission to fulfill. The same spirit of prayer and total commitment is needed to be the kind of church where God's Spirit woos sinners into His kingdom, where miracles of grace occur, and where God's people are built up in the faith.

That is our mission!

Back to Basics: Saved by Grace

Acts 15:1-12

Standing in echoing, hollow-sounding empty churches in Europe, I was reminded that the heart of Christianity once beat there with vitality and life. Impressions etched on my mind provoked me to study and think about how the Christian faith got so deeply entangled with culture and so interwoven with state institutions that it faded from view. Today's evangelical movement calls the Church back to the basics of our Christian faith. What really counts?

A generation of declining comprehension scores and reading levels cries for us to go back to basics in school—reading, writing, and arithmetic. A generation of young adults has produced many who cannot sound out a word or spell in their native tongue. Journalists agree that we must get back to basics.

Many persons have opted for the easy way out, searching for instant solutions. Society is filled with lonely people convinced that anything is right if it feels good. An epidemic of broken homes is rampant because couples have forgotten solemn vows. Americans have filled their houses with stuff, filled their hours with distractions, and filled their thoughts with fantasies and preoccupations. No wonder the family is choked to death!

It's time to lay aside trivia and get back to basics. I've stood beside a lot of sickbeds and deathbeds. Believe me, when the shades are drawn and the curtain is coming down, very little counts but family, close friends, and good influences. I beg you to come back to basics!

Modern humanism and shallow, cheap Christianity haven't worked out. Disillusionment in our day brings renewed opportunity for the real Christian. People are beginning to listen. They are looking for answers. Many are returning to Christ after years of defection. Let's get them grounded on Christian basics that count and really make a difference.

In Acts 15 the church had to face the issue of getting back to basics. The Christian faith had leap-frogged from city to city, from country to country, and from culture to culture. Differences of emphasis began to emerge. Cultural differences arose: "Some men came down from Judea to Antioch and were teaching the brothers: 'Unless you are circumcised, according to the custom taught by Moses [Jewish cultural customs], you cannot be saved'" (v. 1). That issue precipitated the first major controversy of the Early Church. It forced Christians to get back to basics.

Jewish Christians confused their culture with their faith in Christ. They failed to distinguish between the two. Gentiles were becoming Christians but were not becoming Jewish in culture. Circumcision was the outward identification of a Jew with the old covenant. Jewish Christians assumed everyone had to get religion and react the same way they did. Therefore, they labeled Gentile Christians as "unsaved." They insisted that faith in Jesus was not enough—circumcision had to be added.

William Sanford LaSor put it succinctly:

> Must a Gentile become a Jew in order to become a Christian?

51

We are amused by the question today. That is because we are a Gentile Church. But turn the question around: Must a Jew become a Gentile in order to become a Christian? Must an Oriental become a Westerner in order to become a Christian? Must a [black man] become a white man in order to become a Christian? Basically, the question is one of second-class citizens in the kingdom of God. Shall there be in the Church of Christ two groups: those who are saved and in addition . . . keep [certain customs], and those inferior ones who are merely saved? Shall we erect a partition down the middle of the Church and put signs over the doors, admitting . . . special-class members to the one side and relegating . . . second-class members to the other?[1]

When we say, "You must accept Jesus Christ as Savior and you must ———," whatever we think should be written in that blank is the same old problem of the Judaizers! Whatever we insist should be filled in the blank erects barriers and hindrances. We need to learn to accept people as Jesus does— just as they are. Sometimes, said Ogilvie, "like the Judaizers, we have our own convictions about life which we hold as dearly as we do Christ. . . . The Judaizers had Moses, the Law, and circumcision; we have patterns, practices, and prejudices."[2]

"This brought Paul and Barnabas into sharp dispute and debate with them" (v. 2). The unity of the church was threatened. Divisions in churches rarely occur over basics of the Christian faith. Dissension nearly always arises over cultural differences.

Three congregations of one denomination were located at a crossroad—one on each corner. They never cooperated but always competed. Instead of revival meetings, they had rival meetings. One hot, summer night all the windows of the three sanctuaries were open. One congregation began singing "Will There Be Any Stars in My Crown?" The next church started singing loudly "No, Not One." Smugly, the third congregation sang "That Will Be Glory for Me."

But dissension has to be addressed. "So Paul and Barnabas were appointed, along with some other believers, to go up to Jerusalem to see the apostles and elders about this question. The church sent them on their way" (vv. 2-3) and upon their arrival, a Jerusalem Council was called to listen to reports and questions concerning God's work throughout His Church. This first general assembly met around A.D. 48-49. The general assembly journal minutes could be summarized:

Acts 15:5	Introduction of business and debate
15:6-11	Report of Peter's speech
15:12	Summary of corroborating witness of Barnabas and Paul
15:13-21	Report of James' speech
15:22-29	The apostolic letter[3]

An issue begun in hot debate concluded with a call for the Church to move back to basics. The great burden to force everyone into a certain cultural mold was laid aside. God had already been "saving Gentiles without asking anybody's permission . . . and He was doing it without any ritual, or . . . reference to the law of Moses . . . God was already doing what they said could not be done . . . thus God was overruling them."[4] The whole meeting ended on a good note.

From the pulpit of my church, Reuben Welch said, "If God's purpose is to unify, I must be wrong if I seek to divide." Sinners saved by grace are unified in Christ. Homes are unified in Christ. Churches are unified in Christ. Communities are unified in Christ. Whatever divides in spirit must be wrong and must be opposed.

A passenger on a Mississippi River steamboat in the old days said, "Captain, I suppose you know every sandbar in the river."

Replied the captain, "No, I don't. That would be a waste of time."

"What? A waste of time?" exclaimed the passenger. "If you don't know where the sandbars are, how can you pilot the boat?"

"Like I said, 'A waste of time,'" the captain repeated. "Why should I go kicking about among the sandbars? I know where the deep waters run."

Acts 15 doesn't "go kicking about" theological or cultural sandbars. It moves right into the mainstream currents, out where the deep things run—the basics that really count. Amid the debate and speeches in Acts 15 are three basic principles of Christian life and experience.

The first basic principle upon which to build your Christian life states, "We are saved by graced alone." Peter said, "We believe it is through the grace of our Lord Jesus that we are saved, just as they are" (v. 11). This is Peter's last recorded statement in the Book of Acts—but what a way to go! "Saved by grace!"

Saved by Grace, We Are Justified by God

Our own sin separates us from God. We build our own barriers against God. Sin after sin, rebellion after rebellion muffles our ears to God's call of love. Out of harmony with God, we are in discord with ourselves and with others around us.

Man has tried many ways to get back to a wholesome relationship with God. A man says, "I'll be a better person," only to discover himself habitually bound to a fallen nature. He desires to do one thing but finds himself doing what he hates. He says, "I'll be a better husband," only to find his inner nature too selfish to improve. He says, "I'll try harder," only to repeat with increased intensity the same errors, getting less results.

Typical of man's efforts, the Judaizers in Acts 15 were saying, "Religion means earning God's favor by keeping the Law." The Law describes how destitute our souls really are.

54

We seem to have the inherent impulse to contribute to our own salvation. We want to do something to get ourselves into a right relationship with God. As the rich young ruler, we ask insistently, "What good thing must I *do* to get eternal life?" (Matt. 19:16, italics added).

Karl Demel, a tailor in a Vienna prison, sewed for himself a guard's uniform, put it on, and walked right through the front gate to freedom! Karl found his way to freedom by the work of his own hands.

But that can never happen in God's kingdom. Jesus Christ came into this world to set prisoners free from sin and self. And if He sets us free, we are free indeed! Jesus comes to us with liberating assurance: "He saved us, not because of righteous things we had done, but because of his mercy" (Titus 3:5). We are saved by grace alone! All we can do is accept the free gift of God's grace.

The Good News speaks of God's grace. Peter's speech emphasizes, "Religion consists in throwing ourselves on the grace of God." We are saved by grace alone: "For God did not send his Son into the world to condemn the world, but to save the world through him" (John 3:17). God alone can justify us—put us into a right relationship with Him. Justification has already been done at the Cross.

As Ogilvie put it, "Peter wanted the church to remember that the level ground of grace was the only sure footing beneath all Christians, Hebrew and Gentile alike. No one in the church had an edge. Faith was the only open door through which they all had to pass. And that was not their achievement, but God's gift."[5]

Saved by Grace, We Have a New Direction

Headed off in the direction of our impulses, careless decisions, self-serving ambitions, life eventually goes sour. Sooner or later it sows the seeds of its own destruction. But Jesus calls for us to come to Him. By our *repentance* and *confession* of our sins to Him—those good old words for agreeing with God's estimate of us as sinners—God turns us around in a different, new direction. Life takes on meaning. The mirage of fleeting happiness is replaced by deep currents of joy. One fellow described the radical change of his conversion, "My life has turned 180 degrees."

The Word of God says, "I will instruct you and teach you in the way you should go" (Ps. 32:8). And the Psalmist responded, "You have made known to me the path of life; you will fill me with joy in your presence, with eternal pleasures at your right hand" (Ps. 16:11).

Saved by Grace, We Experience a New Birth

During a crusade, a woman came forward with her 16-year-old son. The counselor prayed with the young man and then turned to the mother, "And what about you?"

She replied, "Oh, I've always been a Christian!"

That was the counselor's clue—no one has "always been a Christian." Instead, one has always been a sinner and separated from God until saved by grace. To an impeccably good man, Nicodemus, Jesus insisted, "You must be born again" (John 3:7).

Paul wrote, "If anyone is in Christ, he is a new creation" (2 Cor. 5:17). Later, writing to the churches of Galatia, Paul reminded them of the controversy in Acts 15. He added, "Neither circumcision nor uncircumcision means anything; what counts is a new creation" (Gal. 6:15). In all instances referring to the "new" life in Christ, a certain Greek word was used. The Greeks have two words for "new." *Neos* means "new in reference to time." *Kainos* means "new in terms of quality." A *neos* life or *neos* birth would mean a new beginning of the old way, repeating the same patterns. It suggests a new start, a new beginning. But the New Testament never uses *neos* in the context of "new life in Christ." *Kainos* is used, meaning a new quality of life, a birth or beginning of a different quality. Only

56

Christ can add the dimension of newness to life, which is a life-changing quality.

Robert Howarth listened to a sermon by Billy Graham. He responded and went forward. A young man talked with him briefly, but Robert started away in a fog of confusion. Suddenly a man looked him in the eye and asked, "Are you a Christian?"

Putting on his best Sunday School smile, Robert said, "Oh, yes, I think so."

The man repeated, "Are you a Christian?"

Robert thought the fellow must be a crank. He would humor him and leave. "Well, I'm trying to be."

The man asked, "Ever try to be an elephant?"

Robert testified later, "He took me by the arm, sat me in a chair and explained that no amount of trying could ever transform me into a Christian, any more than it could turn me into an elephant. Then he began to teach me what New Testament Christianity was all about: That Jesus Christ had died in my place. That He had paid the full penalty which my sins demanded. As I was, I stood condemned before a holy God. I needed a Savior. Jesus alone could save me. Forgiveness for the past was possible in Him. Moreover, in His resurrection, He was offering me power to live the sort of life I had . . . considered hopelessly out of reach.

"What a stupendous offer! God was really asking to come into my wretched, tarnished life. I flung open the door. He was as good as His Word."[6]

"We believe it is through the grace of our Lord Jesus that we are saved" (v. 11). Paul added later, "For it is by grace you have been saved, through faith—and this not from yourselves, it is *the gift of God*" (Eph. 2:8, italics added). There's enough in that announcement to change your life! Here again is the first basic principle: We are saved by grace alone.

Back to Basics: Purified by Faith

Acts 15:4-11

Acts 15 underscores three basic principles. The first principle is: *We are saved by grace alone.* "We believe it is through the grace of our Lord Jesus that we are saved" (v. 11). The second principle is: *We are purified by faith alone.* "God, who knows the heart, showed that he accepted them by giving the Holy Spirit to them, just as he did to us. He made no distinction between us and them, for he purified their hearts by faith" (vv. 8-9).

Being saved by grace is more than an occasion, a moment to clear up past sins and failures. More than a crisis experience, conversion is the beginning of our restoration to wholeness, the beginning of our continuing walk with God, the beginning of a new quality of life through the residing presence of Christ in us.

A wedding is a moment in time when two people come together to pledge a covenant relationship. But the wedding is only the beginning of a marriage. The wedding has little value unless followed by a marriage relationship. Our conversion experience weds us to Christ, but our continuing joy comes from the ongoing relationship with Him. Conversion has little lasting value if it isn't followed by a deepening, enriching relationship with God.

Purified by Faith, We Are Sanctified by the Holy Spirit

God has the answer: "God, who knows the heart ...
[gave] the Holy Spirit to them ... for he purified their hearts
by faith" (vv. 8-9). The Bible often uses the word "sanctify" to
describe God's purifying work in our hearts. The dictionary
defines "sanctify" as "(1) make holy; (2) set apart as sacred,
observe as holy; (3) make free from sin." Sanctification is a
basic biblical concept. The word "sanctify" and its derivatives
are used more than 141 times in Scripture.

Holiness as purity or cleansing runs through much Old
Testament teaching. Whatever was claimed by God as holy
and dedicated for His service was sanctified or cleansed and
kept from defilement. Holiness as purity or cleansing is prom-
inent in the New Testament. Jesus said, "Blessed are the pure
in heart, for they will see God" (Matt. 5:8). Jesus "loved the
church and gave himself up for her to make her holy, cleansing her ... to present her to himself ... holy and blameless"
(Eph. 5:25-27).

Under the Law consecrated things were first sprinkled
with blood and then anointed with oil. They were then set
apart for holy use. Under the gospel every Christian has been
sprinkled with the blood of Jesus and then anointed by the
Holy Spirit. He is then separated for holy use and consecrated
to God.

Peter argued at the Jerusalem Council that God had
made Gentile Christians in Cornelius' house holy and pure
just as He did the apostles on the Day of Pentecost in Jerusalem: "He made no distinction between us and them, for he
purified their hearts by faith" (Acts 10).

Peter himself had experienced a great cleansing, a purifying of his heart at Pentecost (Acts 2). He knew God had
done a great work in him. From the depths of his denials of
Jesus out of fear, Peter's heart had been cleansed and filled
with the Holy Spirit until he could stand publicly and speak

59

God's Word boldly. Peter's vascillating spirit was purified into a victorious spirit by the indwelling Spirit of God. Now Peter reminds the Jerusalem Council that God still cleanses the hearts of new Christians everywhere.

God works in response to man's faith: "purifying their hearts by faith." Faith is volitional, not emotional: "I will believe!" "I will trust God to keep His promise!" "I do accept His cleansing!" Faith takes a mighty leap into God's arms and makes a mighty commitment to God. John Wesley said faith "is both the condition and the instrument of [sanctification]. When we begin to believe, then sanctification begins. And as faith increases, holiness increases, till we are created anew."[1]

Judy Mueting, a young growing Christian, commented in her Sunday School class, "When I was saved, I knew I was prepared for eternity, but I needed the Holy Spirit to prepare me for living here and now!"

God's enabling power for "here and now" is the Holy Spirit coming in response to our faith in order to cleanse and set up housekeeping and to preside in our hearts. God has left nothing undone! He commands us to be pure and holy because His reputation is at stake in our lives if we call ourselves "Christian"!

Purified by Faith, We Have a Change of Nature

When forgiven by God, all our old acts of sin are stricken from God's recording files. Nothing in our past can be brought against us before God. However, if our inner nature remains the same, eventually acts of sin, expressions of our old inner nature, will occur again and again.

I might knock all the lemons off my tree and tie on huge, juicy oranges. People would see the fruit and say, "My, what a wonderful orange tree." But eventually the old lemon nature will express itself in sour lemons. It's just a lemon tree with dead oranges—the sour nature is still there.

Our selfish moral nature is sour. Dr. James Kennedy said, "We don't like it and we resolve to do better. We try to throw away the fruits of our sour nature. We get rid of the bottle, clean up our language (except under unexpected emergencies) and try to better our family and business relationships. . . . We get rid of bad habits and acquire good ones. All we are really doing is picking off lemons and sticking on oranges. However, . . . the source of the stream of life [is not changed]. Our nature is untouched by our resolutions and [good intentions]. We are as powerless to make our hearts good as we are to make a lemon tree into an orange tree."[2]

I wish all Christians were as afraid of sin in their lives as they seem to be afraid of holiness—or as afraid of imperfect lives as they are of perfect love. One fellow exclaimed, "Well, you can't be a walking saint, can you?" That's the only kind you can be—a walking saint: "But if we walk in the light, as he is in the light, we have fellowship with one another, and the blood of Jesus, his Son, purifies us from all sin" (1 John 1:7). The Bible says, "That the righteousness of the law might be fulfilled in us, who walk not after the flesh, but after the Spirit" (Rom. 8:4, KJV). God's solution includes a change of nature: saints with pure hearts instead of sinners with a forgiven past!

God purifies the heart of His child in response to faith. The Bible says, "But just as he who called you is holy, so be holy in all you do; for it is written: 'Be holy, because I am holy'" (1 Pet. 1:15-16). We are to have God's nature in us. Having been delivered from guilt and the power of sin, we are given a new nature. This nature is God's nature, only in smaller measure. A spark of fire is like fire. The tiniest branch on a giant sequoia tree has the same nature as the huge, giant General Sherman tree. A glass of ocean water is like the ocean—not in size, but in essence. A sanctified person is holy like God—not all-powerful, not omnipotent, not all-wise—but his nature is like God's—good, pure, loving. The Bible says, "His divine power has given us everything we need for life and godliness through our knowledge of him who called us by his own glory and goodness. Through these he has given us his very great and precious promises, so that through them you may participate in the divine nature and escape the corruption in the world caused by evil desires" (2 Pet. 1:3-4).

This is Good News! God has a solution for man's fallen nature. Often this great truth has been overlooked. Augustine, fighting the desires of his immoral nature, did not understand that God could deliver from *all* sin. John Calvin regretted his vicious temper but knew no remedy for it. Many Christians doubt salvation from all sin because they wrongly think that sin is in the physical body. The Bible says, "Those controlled by the sinful nature cannot please God" (Rom. 8:8). Physical nature and sinful nature are not the same. Paul defines sinful nature as "hostile to God" (v. 7). Those who confuse sin with the physical body have failed to read on: "You, however, are controlled not by the sinful nature but by the Spirit, if the Spirit of God lives in you" (v. 9).

When God purifies our hearts by faith, He gives us a new nature—cleansing and filling until rebellion is removed from our hearts.

Purified by Faith, We Have a Cleansed Heart

Holiness brings spiritual wholeness or inner health. The English words *holy* and *health* come from the same Anglo-Saxon root. Not all problems are solved when our hearts are purified by faith, but inner conflicts begin to resolve in the heart devoted to God. God said, "I will cleanse you from all your impurities and from all your idols. I will give you a new heart and put a new spirit in you; I will remove from you your heart of stone and give you a heart of flesh" (Ezek. 36:25-26).

Sadly, some well-meaning Christians think the Bible teaches that the sinful heart remains through life. To them, the best God can do is help hold down the lid of self-restraint so acts of sin won't spring from the heart. How disappointing for those who hunger and thirst after God's righteousness! How despairing to think that God was only teasing with His call to holiness! The only other way to resolve inner conflict is either by watering down the awfulness of sin or explaining away the holiness of God! God's solution is a new nature—a heart free from hostility to God!

A missionary told a story to a group in India:

A big, deadly snake entered into a house and lived in a hole in the wall. The family, knowing about it, lived in fear. They asked neighbors, "What shall we do?"

One neighbor advised, "Have your house white-washed."

Another suggested, "Have a carpenter repair all the doors and windows."

A third neighbor urged, "Send for a Brahmin to utter a sacred voice."

The family did everything suggested and finally slept in peace. But one night the snake crawled out of his hole and bit the father who died shortly after. Two nights later, the son was bitten and he, too, died.

Then the missionary looked right into the eyes of his audience and asked, "Do you know the meaning of this parable? The house is your body. The hole is your heart. The snake is sin. By all your sayings and ceremonies you will no more get sin out of your heart than that sad family got the snake out by whitewash and paint and rituals. Jesus is the only remedy for sin!"

The Bible says, "If we confess our sins, he is faithful and just and will forgive us our sins and purify us from all un-righteousness" (1 John 1:9). His purifying work cleans out the sinful nature. He gives us a pure heart. The beauty of holiness is not in a cleansed, vacant heart but in the holy presence of God's indwelling Spirit.

63

A cartoon in my files shows a boy in a bathtub. His toys are jammed into that bathtub right up to his chin. His mother is reaching down into the tub and says, "Aha! Just as I suspected—no water!"

We are so cluttered with stuff—business matters, leisure activities, and even religious toys—that we neglect our opportunity for God's cleansing. He alone can purify and fill us with His Spirit. Keep the channels of your heart open to the cleansing work of the Holy Spirit.

At my uncle's house no water would come out of the faucets. Though the tap turned, nothing happened—no water. A plumber came and examined all the fittings and connections. Everything seemed all right—plenty of water in the reservoir, every piece of equipment properly installed—but still no water. Finally, one pipe was pulled up and examined. A dead mouse was found!

There's no use turning the tap—singing, praising, testifying—if there's something between you and God, if there's something corrupt you're holding back from God, if there's something troubling your conscience, if there's something you refuse to give up, if there's something blocking the channel of communication between you and God. You'll not experience the Holy Spirit's cleansing. He won't remain in a defiled heart. You must confess it, give it up, and surrender it to the Lord. Only then can you know and experience God's cleansing, purifying grace.

Being purified by faith is a possibility for every Christian. The Bible says, "Be filled with the Spirit" (Eph. 5:18). Every Christian is commanded to be filled with God's Spirit. To ignore or disregard God's filling is to be disobedient to His command and to walk behind light in your own soul.

When God commands us to be filled with His Spirit, we can be assured that He has power to cleanse and fill us the very moment we invite Him by faith to do so. God, who knows the heart, will purify your heart by faith!

Back to Basics:
Restricted by Love

Acts 15:12-35

The council of Jerusalem met to decide how to settle cultural differences between Christians of the Greek world and Christians of Jewish background. After debates and reports, Peter made a closing speech. It contained two basics for the Christian faith: The first principle: *We are saved by grace* (see v. 11). The second principle: *We are purified by faith* (see vv. 8-9).

James, brother of Jesus, saw Old Testament prophecy fulfilled in the conversion of Gentiles. He concluded: "It is my judgment, therefore, that we should not make it difficult for the Gentiles who are turning to God. Instead we should write to them, telling them to abstain from foods polluted by idols, from sexual immorality, from the meat of strangled animals and from blood. For Moses has been preached in every city from the earliest times and is read in the synagogues on every Sabbath" (vv. 19-21).

The council drew up a letter and appointed men to take the letter to all the churches, explaining and answering questions so that no misunderstanding could arise. Here's the letter:

The apostles and elders, your brothers,
To the Gentile believers in Antioch, Syria and Cilicia:

65

Greetings,

We have heard that some went out from us without our authorization and distrubed you, troubling your minds by what they said. So we all agreed to choose some men and send them to you with our dear friends Barnabas and Paul—men who have risked their lives for the name of our Lord Jesus Christ. Therefore we are sending Judas and Silas to confirm by word of mouth what we are writing. It seemed good to the Holy Spirit and to us not to burden you with anything beyond the following requirements: You are to abstain from food sacrificed to idols, from blood, from the meat of strangled animals and from sexual immorality. You will do well to avoid these things. Farewell *(vv. 23-29)*.

The letter carried a basic principle suggested by the four restrictions passed on to the Gentile church. Two restrictions were in the moral realm—idolatry and sexual immorality. Two restrictions were in the realm of sensitivity and understanding toward feelings of Jewish Christians—meat from strangled animals and drinking blood.

The matters of moral significance, idolatry and sexual immorality, were universal moral restrictions clearly expressed in God's Word. These typical sins of Gentile culture violated God's universal moral law, the Ten Commandments. In Jewish thinking, idolatry, sexual immorality, and murder were three cardinal sins. From Noah's time, hundreds of years before the giving of the Ten Commandments, the prohibition of these three sins was binding on the human race. Later, in A.D. 135, rabbis from Lydda taught that a Jew could break any commandment of the Law if his life were at stake—except idolatry, sexual sin, and murder.

One of the problems faced by early Christians was meat offered to idols. When a heathen sacrificed to pagan gods, only a small part was kept at the temple. The remainder he took to sell or make a feast for his friends—often inviting

Christian friends. Christians felt convicted knowingly feasting on meat offered to idols. The Early Church agreed to avoid it.

Abstinence from sexual immorality was in contrast to pagan cultures. Someone has said that chastity was the only new virtue Christianity brought into the world. In spite of allurements, Christians must remain pure in an impure world. To describe fornication or sexual immorality, James used the Greek word, *porneias,* from which our English word *pornography* comes. The term includes the practice of premarital sex, adultery, all sorts of incestuous relationships, and particularly prostitution, which was so much a part of pagan temples in that era. Christians are not to violate another person's integrity or use one another as things!

The second group of restrictions in the letter were matters of sensitivity and scruples. Out of compassion and reverence for life, Jews would not eat or drink blood. James wanted all Christians to reverence life—and to avoid making even animals suffer the torture of strangulation. The Old Testament taught, "But you must not eat meat that has its life-blood still in it" (Gen. 9:4). It became a matter of scruples with the Jews. They equated life with blood—its hard to get along without it! All meat for Jewish tables was drained of blood, for blood was life and life belongs to God. Thus, these scruples were deeply engrained in the Jewish conscience.

As a leader in the church, James concluded that Jewish Christians should not impose all the details of Jewish cultural law upon Gentile Christians. However, James insisted, Gentile Christians should respect their Jewish brethren's scruples by avoiding these things and rejecting the low moral standards of the pagan world. These suggestions were guidelines for a clean, moral life as well as an avenue for building the bonds of love between all Christians—Jewish and Gentile. After all, the letter was from "brothers" to "brothers." The Holy Spirit had guided them toward concern for new Gentile converts and counseled new believers toward sensitivity about

67

the feelings of others. These attitudes are necessary for growing in the Lord.

The Church was called back to basics of the faith: saved by grace, purified by faith, and the apostolic letter underscores the third principle: *We are restricted by love.*

Christians are free to do anything but violate love! Anything that hurts and hinders love is wrong. That's the essence of James' letter: "We don't want to lay unnecessary burdens on you. We don't expect you to have our cultural background. Since you are saved by grace and purified by faith, you are free to do as you like—except hurt love. These moral matters hurt love—hurt God, others, and yourself! Love is concerned for another person's scruples." But peer pressure is love's deadly foe, pushing you to violate your scruples and ideals. It is the insidious enemy of your highest and best interests.

Sensitivity to love others and to love God are the Christian's only restrictions. Faith is the soul's intake; love is the soul's outlet. Faith makes things possible; love makes things worthwhile.

A person saved by grace and purified in his heart by faith will be concerned to not be a stumbling block nor to live inconsistent with biblical standards. He desires to live above reproach for Jesus' sake. He does not have perfect insight or judgment, but his heart would not choose to offend love. Restricted by love, he cares what happens to people. He cares if his conduct hurts or hinders. One girl wrote, "Poverty is what happens when people stop caring for one another." Genuine Christians desire to reach out in love to one another.

In Christ, We Are Motivated by Love

Justified by God and purified by the Holy Spirit, Jesus motivates us by love. Love purifies the heart from selfishness. We are restricted by love alone!

If we love, then why do we require so much of people before we accept them? Dr. Lloyd Ogilvie noted, "We may have more rigid requirements than the Lord! His love has no strings!"[1] Getting back to basics, we need to examine our secondary cultural requirements. Sometimes our own brand of Christian experience or church organization becomes more important than Jesus. If we are not careful, "Our customs may become more crucial than the truth they were established to maintain."[2] Ogilvie added, "We all run the danger of listening for our own language or of putting people through the paces of our heritage before we accept them as brothers and sisters with unqualified love. Many powerful movements in Christian history began with an emphasis which was liberating but later incarcerated potential participants. ... The emphasis was excellent, but when it became more important than Christ, it became exclusive."[3]

Restricted only by love, we are motivated to accept others and serve them for Jesus. Dr. Mildred Wynkoop wrote, "The dynamic of personal relationship is love. Love is a quality of response between persons. Love can exist only in freedom. It cannot be coerced. Freedom is the most fundamental ingredient of love."[4]

In life you face ultimately two freedoms: the false—free to do what you like; and the true—free to do what you ought. That's the restriction of love—free to do as you ought!

Paul explained love's motivation in dealing with people:

I am not bound to obey anyone just because he pays my salary; yet I have freely and happily become a servant of any and all so that I can win them to Christ. When I am with the Jews I seem as one of them so that they will listen to the Gospel and I can win them to Christ. When I am with Gentiles who follow Jewish customs and ceremonies I don't argue, even though I don't agree, because I want to help them. When with the heathen I agree with them as much as I can, except of course that I must always do what is right as a Chris-

69

tian. And so, by agreeing, I can win their confidence and help them too.

When I am with those whose consciences bother them easily, I don't act as though I know it all and don't say they are foolish; the result is that they are willing to let me help them. Yes, whatever a person is like, I try to find common ground with him so that he will let me tell him about Christ and let Christ save him. I do this to get the Gospel to them and also for the blessing I myself receive when I see them come to Christ *(1 Cor. 9:19-23, TLB).*

Paul was motivated by Christ's love!

Restricted by Love, Our Conduct Changes

Becoming Christian, we got a change of direction. Being cleansed by the Holy Spirit, we got a change of nature. Governed by love, we get a change of conduct. Our actions express love. Our daily lives are different because pure hearts overflow with compassion and love. Clean hearts demonstrate responsible love.

James' letter called for new believers to live without offense to others. Unbelievers lived for self and sometimes new converts carried old habits over into the church. James warned all new converts to avoid the polluting influences of pagan cultures. He asked them not to offend the sensibilities of other Christians, but to make a clean break with their past.

If we're not careful, we forget that love is the only restriction placed on the new convert. Ogilvie noted, "We all have value systems which we try to baptize into sanctified importance. Education, background, habits of dress, codes of ethics, and standards of living often become a legacy that we bring into the Christian life and use to Judaize people."[5]

While you should hold great convictions about truth, you must also have great respect for people. The Council of Jerusalem called the Church back to basics. Few things really matter deeply. These things you must uphold with total commitment. All else must be restricted by love alone. Thomas Jefferson said, "In matters of principle, stand like a rock. In matters of taste, swim with the current!"

One pastor noted, "In the Kingdom of God we first love, then we move into acquaintance. In this world we first get acquainted, then we move into love sometimes. As a result, most people have many acquaintances and few friends, but they are dying from lack of love."[6]

Born into the family of God, you find many opportunities to express love—and you get acquainted as you grow in the community of believers. Jesus told His fledgling church: "A new commandment I give you: Love one another. As I have loved you, so you must love one another. All men will know that you are my disciples if you love one another" (John 13:34-35).

Our behavior should demonstrate love. We should treat our marriage partner, children, and neighbors as Jesus would. We are restricted only by love. Edwin Markham put it graphically:

> *He drew a circle that shut me out—*
> *Heretic, rebel, a thing to flout.*
> *But Love and I had the wit to win:*
> *We drew a circle that took him in!*

Restricted by Love, Our Conduct Has New Controls

Conversion is our new birth. Cleansing gives us a new heart. As a result, our conduct has new controls. How does love act? "Love is patient, love is kind. It does not envy, it does not boast, it is not proud. It is not rude, it is not self-seeking, it is not easily angered, it keeps no record of wrongs. Love does not delight in evil but rejoices with the truth. It always protects, always trusts, always hopes, always perseveres" (1 Cor. 13:4-7).

In our conduct, we are apt to go to two extremes—and both are wrong.

The first extreme is the notion that because you are saved by grace, no rules or regulations limit your conduct. . . .

Actually, Christians *are* free from the Law—they need not obey it to earn salvation. Eternal life is God's gift; we can neither earn it nor keep it by obeying the Law or any other rules.

But God expects His children to obey Him—not so that they may be saved but *because they have been saved.* . . .

The other of the two extremes is legalism. Some earnest Christians lack an adequate conception of the completeness of Christ's sacrifice. They feel that though they have been saved by faith, they are made more spiritual by living according to certain [man-made] rules. . . . They sometimes depend largely on negatives. By not engaging in certain practices they feel they are living "separated" lives. That *can* be legalism.[7]

Unfortunately, legalists, like Judaizers in the Book of Acts, feel compelled to force everyone into their cultural mold. When others disagree with them, they react like graduates of the "Don Rickles School of Charm."

The Jerusalem council sent its letter to urge Christians to consider the conscience and spiritual well-being of others—and voluntarily let love restrict their personal freedom in order to help others. Love restricts not by coercion but by free choice.

As one writer stated, "Acts 15 shows us that Christians have freedom. It also shows us that they have obligations to others. They are not to turn their liberty into license or give offense to other believers. Christian liberty is important, but so is Christian love."[8] We are restricted by love alone!

What was the result of calling the church back to basics? "The men were sent off and went down to Antioch, where they gathered the church together and delivered the letter. The people read it and were glad for its encouraging message" (vv.

30-31). The church began to grow once again. Love results in impartial goodwill.

As we get down to basics, barriers are broken down. "We believe it is through the grace of our Lord Jesus that we are saved, just as they are" (v. 11). We are saved by grace. "God . . . accepted them by giving the Holy Spirit to them, just as he did to us. He made no distinction between us and them, for he purified their hearts by faith" (vv. 8-9). We are purified by faith. As a consequence, we are restricted by love.

Immediately following the Civil War, a Black man thought that the end of the war had abolished the degrading experience of discrimination. Believing himself equal under the law, he entered an all-white church to worship.

People were surprised and shocked. Some moved away from the former slave.

The worship service progressed slowly, but without much freedom. Finally the pastor called for the people to come to the Lord's Supper to share Holy Communion. In his invitation, he reminded the people that they were one at the Lord's Table.

The Black man was first to respond. He knelt at the altar—but no one else moved. The silence hung heavy until finally a tall gentleman near the back stood up, came forward, and knelt beside the Black man. The two were one in Christ at the Lord's Table.

At the close of the Lord's Supper, the Black man and General Robert E. Lee walked back together to their respective pews.

We are one in the bond of love. Our actions are restricted only by love.

"Dear friends, let us love one another, for love comes from God. Everyone who loves has been born of God and knows God. Whoever does not love does not know God, because God is love. This is how God showed his love among us: He sent his one and only Son into the world that we might live

73

through him. This is love: not that we loved God, but that he loved us and sent his Son as an atoning sacrifice for our sins. Dear friends, since God so loved us, we also ought to love one another. . . . if we love each other, God lives in us and his love is made complete in us" (1 John 4:7-12).

Make Use of Your Mistakes

Acts 15:36-41

A church sign said, "We never lose if we learn from losing."

A new college student craved to be a leader. He ran for freshman class president but was badly defeated. His name was John F. Kennedy.

One young man aspired to be a military officer or statesman. He failed his student entrance exams three times for the Royal Military College. His name was Winston Churchill.

Having 24 brothers and sisters, one boy lived in terrible poverty. Shuttled from one foster home to another, he finally dropped out of high school at age 16. His name is Flip Wilson.

Wanting to be an actress, she went to dramatics school in New York. Her teacher told her, "You have no acting ability." Her name is Lucille Ball—and she was 40 years old when she began her first "I Love Lucy Show." At 75 Lucy is beginning a new television series.

For 20 years he held the world's record for strike-outs. One thousand, three hundred and thirty times he stood at home plate, fanned the air, and took that long, humiliating walk back to the bench. His name? Babe Ruth.

Mistakes are the price people pay for going ahead in spite of the possibility of failure. Doing nothing may avoid many mistakes, but is itself the greatest mistake.

The Bible's integrity is enhanced by showing real people —"warts and all!" After portraying Paul in one of his great victories, Luke reported a great mistake in Paul's career.

Leaving the Council of Jerusalem, Paul got concerned for new converts from his previous missionary trip. Deciding to check up on them, he said to Barnabas, "Let us go back and visit the brothers in all the towns where we preached the word of the Lord and see how they are doing" (v. 36). His word for "visit" means "to inspect the troops"!

Plans for this second missionary journey sparked a dispute between Paul and Barnabas. Barnabas insisted on taking John Mark, but Paul refused. He remembered how Mark had quit on their first missionary tour.

This contradiction of honest judgment shows what can happen when good men disagree. Even with the mistake, conflict of keen minds and strong personalities is better than indifferent acquiescence of apathetic minds and weak personalities. Anyone doing something will make mistakes.

Learn to make use of your mistakes—that draws the fear out of failure.

A news wire service had an item titled "Secretary Made Millions Hiding Errors from Boss."

If anyone ever profited from her own mistakes, it was Bette Claire Graham.

> A bank secretary and a free-lance artist, Mrs. Graham concocted in her kitchen in 1954 a fluid to paint over her typing errors.
>
> Using her knowledge of pigments and solvents, she "put some tempera waterbase paint in a bottle and took my watercolor brush to the office and used that to correct my mistakes," according to a recent interview.
>
> She kept the invention to herself, but two years later the liquid she called "Mistake Out" was being used by all the secretaries in her building and an office supply dealer urged her to market it.

But marketing agencies weren't impressed and she decided to sell the fluid on her own.

She formed Liquid Paper Corporation and in a few months was filling orders from around the company for the tiny bottles of white paint equipped with a small brush.

Mrs. Graham died . . . at age 56 of an undisclosed illness having sold the firm . . . to the Gillette Company for $47.5 million.

At the time of her death those tiny white bottles were earning $3.5 million annually on sales of $38 million.[1]

There's a lady who learned to make use of her mistakes—and mine!

What can we do with our mistakes? In our efforts to serve God, how do we deal with inevitable mistakes?

We Must Accept the Fact That We Will Make Mistakes Even Though Our Hearts Are Right with God

Some people are shocked to discover that even though they love God and eagerly try to follow God's will they make mistakes. Christian perfection taught in the Bible means purity of heart, not perfection of performance.

An airline company got concerned over the rising percentage of accidents. At last they eliminated human error by building a completely automatic computerized airplane.

On its maiden flight the jet engines pushed it into the sky. A voice came over the loudspeakers: "Ladies and gentlemen, it may interest you to know that you are now traveling in the world's first completely automatic passenger airplane. Sit back and relax, for nothing can go wrong—go wrong—go wrong—!"

When trying to walk like saints above, there's nothing like a good brash mistake to get your feet back on the ground. There's no need to pretend "all is well" when you've made a horrendous blooper. Don't act as though nothing went wrong.

Don't soft-pedal it by giving your mistake a different name. Face up to it.

A newly rich Texan went into a Rolls Royce showroom. With his most subtle salespitch, the salesman steered him to the most expensive car on the floor. The Texan remarked, "Well, she's a mighty nice-looking car, but what if she breaks down?"

The low-key salesman straightened up and replied, "Sir, a Rolls Royce never breaks down. It just fails to proceed."

When our humanity "fails to proceed," it is not a sin. Some folk get sins and mistakes mixed up. A mistake is not a sin. A sin is not a mistake. A mistake comes from the head. Sin proceeds from an evil desire in the heart. A rebellious choice and a bad spirit motivate sin; neither is involved in a mistake. Mistakes may have serious results, yet one is innocent of sin. A mistaken idea may lead to a mistake in conduct. Unless a person discovers his mistake in time to become responsible, he is not guilty of sin. Sin is rebellion; a mistake is an error.

Spirit-filled Christians may not always exercise good judgment.

Paul failed to see the worth of a person: "Barnabas wanted to take John, also called Mark, with them, but Paul did not think it wise to take him, because he had deserted them in Pamphylia and had not continued with them in the work" (vv. 37-38). There's an interesting variation in the two Greek verbs for "to take." Barnabas wishes to take Mark at this moment—a completed act. Barnabas saw it as a decision of the moment. Paul wished not to take Mark—having him along day after day. Paul saw it as a decision with ongoing consequences. After all, Mark had been unreliable. Paul couldn't overlook Mark's past failure in order to see his present worth. Paul had set high standards of conduct and character for himself; he would not settle for less in others—especially Mark.

What differences show up—Paul a man of principle and Barnabas a man of people! Stedman commented, "Both . . . men are right! One was looking at the work and the other at the person . . . Paul . . . was . . . right to say, 'We don't want [someone who will quit on us].' And he probably quoted the words of Jesus, 'If any man puts his hand to the plow and turns back, he is not worthy of the kingdom of God.' Christian service and ministry *are* demanding . . . those who [serve] should be prepared to go through with [God's] work and stick with it. . . . God's cause is injured by those who quit in the middle."[2]

Paul failed to be redemptive. He gave no room for a second chance. Burning with zeal he could not sympathize with a quitter. Paul's love for Mark had definite boundaries: "You're a good man, but—!" While Paul's heart was right with God, his judgment was poor.

As usual, Barnabas saw promising qualities in his young kinsman. Surely he would help Mark develop under his guidance. Barnabas was willing to forget past failures. He believed Mark had gifts and qualities God would use. Yes, Mark had failed—once. But who hasn't? The gospel of Jesus has always been the good news of a second chance. One has noted, "The friendship of Barnabas . . . gave Mark back his self-respect. . . . [It] made him determined to make good. The greatest thing a man can have is someone who believes in him."[3]

Paul failed to remember his own recovery by Barnabas. Obviously Paul forgot how Barnabas went out on a limb to back him after his conversion. Barnabas stood up for Paul when his reputation preceded him in Jerusalem. He went to Tarsus, plucked Paul off the shelf, and brought him back after years of obscurity to be his associate pastor in the church at Antioch. Barnabas took Paul along on the first missionary journey and enabled Paul to develop his leadership until the team became known as "Paul and Barnabas." How quickly we can overlook God's grace at work in others that worked so clearly in us!

Spirit-filled Christians are not guaranteed perfect judgment. Based on faulty human judgment, we can make colossal errors.

Spirit-filled Christians may not always exhibit good behavior. While Paul had great character and self-discipline, he could deal with people rather severely. Though he and his ministry brought inspiration and encouragement, he may not have been easy to live with. Limited judgment, stern temperament, and poor health can cause moods, actions, and emotions that appear unChristlike. Some things may affect the mind which in turn affects one's conduct. We must be sympathetic and patient with people's actions—as well as our own. "We have this treasure in earthen vessels" (2 Cor. 4:7, KJV). Let's keep our eyes on Jesus—not on ourselves or the foibles of others.

John Wesley warned, "A man may be filled with pure love, and still liable to mistake. Indeed, I do not expect to be freed from actual mistakes till this mortal puts on immortality."[4]

Paul and Barnabas got into sharp disagreement, "They had such a sharp disagreement that they parted company" (v. 39). Good people attempting to serve God can experience this same tragedy—personality clash. Each believed himself to be absolutely right; neither would give in.

Paul and Barnabas forgot to focus on unity. They overlooked prayer and submission—of which Paul speaks so much in later writings. They overlooked the give-and-take and check-and-balance that protect the members of the body of Christ. An essential unity of love binds our differences in Christ.

You can tie the legs of several chickens together and throw them over a clothesline and have union—but not unity! God had called both Barnabas and Paul to offset each other's strengths and weaknesses. Barnabas was full of kindness, generous to a fault, probably sentimental and too sympathetic, and too easily influenced. Paul was the man of principle—to the point of stubbornness and rigidity. They really needed each other!

Paul and Barnabas should have joined in prayer by which the Holy Spirit could have shown them what to do with John Mark. He had guided them through many other difficult situations. But their actions indicate a lack of mutual understanding. How much we need to learn: "In essentials, unity; in nonessentials, liberty; in all things, charity!"

Yes, God could have prevented them from making such a mistake. But God is too wise for that. Suppose a teacher does not prepare for a Sunday School class. "God may bless the class anyway. But He may also do them a favor by letting the teacher look like an idiot some Sunday just to get him studying again. . . . Failure is the opportunity to grow."[5]

Paul and Barnabas parted company. No doubt they left each other in sorrow. Paul owed so much to Barnabas, and Barnabas was leaving one of history's greatest men. One's good judgment may go with Paul, but one's heart goes with Barnabas. There's something sad when great teams break up—coworkers, marriages, close friends. Mistakes in judgment and behavior sometimes leave great scars though the stain be washed away in God's forgetfulness.

We Must Let God Work Through Us in Spite of Our Mistakes

God can use us in spite of our inadequacies and mistakes. After all, "God chose the foolish things of the world to shame the wise" (1 Cor. 1:27). Though making a mistake of judgment and behavior, Paul did set out on his second missionary tour. No doubt he went with heartache and high hopes mingled.

But from this point on, Paul seems to pray more, to be more sensitive to people, and to speak more of God's unconditional love. After this episode, Paul seems to make sure of God's guidance.

God can overrule the tragic effects of our mistakes. Though such disputes are an embarrassment to the kingdom of God, the Lord brought some good out of it. For one thing, God had two missionary teams instead of one: "Barnabas took Mark and sailed for Cyprus, but Paul chose Silas and left . . . through Syria and Cilicia, strengthening the churches" (vv. 39-41). Second, it was more profitable for Mark to go with Barnabas than to be subjected to Paul's scrutiny. Third, it was profitable for Paul to team up with Silas, a Roman citizen able to travel easily across boundaries. He was a member of the Jerusalem Church sent with the apostolic letter to explain Christian liberty, who became well known in New Testament letters as Silas or Silvanus. Sometimes our mistakes are woven into the beautiful pattern of the Master Architect.

Mistakes do not lessen our standing with God. God can bring glory to himself through all things. Our weaknesses provide opportunities to bring glory to Jesus. Put yourself at God's disposal: "'Lord, when I stand in front of that group Sunday I want people to see you. If falling on my face, stuttering, forgetting my notes will cause people to see you, I am ready. Pull the rug out. I am not trying to gather praise for myself.' . . . A willingness to fail opens all sorts of exciting possibilities. If we are always afraid to fail, then we are not willing to take risks for God."[6]

Let's learn to make use of our mistakes. A whole new world may open up!

We Need to Deal with Our Mistakes as We Realize Them

The perspective of time helped Paul realize his mistaken judgment of Mark and his broken fellowship with Barnabas.

After working with Barnabas, Mark returned to Peter. According to Peter's first letter, Mark was with him in "Babylon" (1 Pet. 5:13). Mark wrote his Gospel as the secretary to Peter. Both Matthew and Luke used Mark's Gospel as an outline and guide for their biographies of Jesus. What an important contribution! Paul and Mark met during Paul's imprisonment in Rome. Paul finally learned to recognize Mark's great worth as he wrote from the Mamertine prison: "Only Luke is with me. Get Mark and bring him with you, because he is helpful to me in my ministry" (2 Tim. 4:11).

There are some practical steps to be taken when we realize our mistakes:

First, we should admit our mistakes to ourselves, to others involved, and to God. The computer is a wonderful invention—there are just as many mistakes as ever, but they are nobody's fault. And they seem impossible to correct.

Abe Lemons, coaching for Texas University, told one of his basketball players: "I can't use you. All the guys hate you."

The player demanded an explanation.

"All right," said Lemons, "I'll tell you. You never think anything is your fault. You always blame somebody else. I've never once heard you say, 'My fault.' In fact, I don't think you can. Why don't you say, 'My fault,' right now—just for practice, just to show you can say it. Now say it: 'My fault!'"

"What for?" said the player. "I didn't do anything."

One who refuses to admit a mistake will resist improvement. He can't make use of his mistakes. Past failure doesn't keep God from trusting me the moment I am ready to try again. God doesn't keep me down just because I fell down once. He lifts me!

Second, we should attempt to mend broken relationships. Too many people take advantage of the fact that it isn't human to be perfect. Paul and Barnabas's struggle is no biblical justification for splintering groups of believers or breaking fellowship with those with whom we don't agree. Ogilvie commented, "This dark paragraph on the pages of Acts does not give us freedom to run roughshod over people because Paul and Barnabas didn't make it. Read the subsequent life of Paul and repeatedly you will find references to his ... efforts to affirm Mark and make up for the qualified love he expressed that day at Antioch."[7] The alienation was not permanent.

Jesus himself taught, "If you are offering your gift at the altar and there remember that your brother has something against you, leave your gift there in front of the altar. First go and be reconciled to your brother; then come and offer your gift" (Matt. 5:23-24).

Third, we should learn from our mistakes. If we don't learn from our mistakes, there's no sense in making them. Samuel Smiles said, "He who never made a mistake never made a discovery."

Thirty-eight tourists swarmed into a quaint little inn at Lake Tahoe. One waiter weaved in and out of the crowded tables, holding up a loaded tray. A lady asked, "How did you learn to carry a tray so skillfully?"

He answered, "I dropped one once!"

Mistakes can make us teachable. Ask God to teach you something. If you don't profit from a mistake, then its wasted. Make use of your mistakes! It's hard to defeat a person who turns mistakes into gain.

Learn from your mistake, determine not to make it again, and forget it!

Fourth, we should draw on God's grace and atonement. Though human error and infirmity are not sin, Christ's atonement covers them all. John Wesley said, "Every such mistake is a transgression of the perfect law. ... The most perfect have continual need of the merits of Christ, even for their actual transgressions, and may say for themselves ... 'Forgive us our trespasses.'"[8] We are dependent upon God's great grace in all of life's shortcomings. You should never drop the ball intentionally to glorify weakness, but don't fear mistakes as though they are the last straw that breaks the camel's back. Allow your mistakes to drink deeply at the fountain of God's grace.

Fifth, we should keep on serving the Lord. In spite of the incident, all those involved in the disagreement and separation kept right on serving Jesus. Barnabas and Mark returned to Barnabas' home area—Cyprus. They disappear from the Book of Acts, but not from God's service. According to tradition, Barnabas worked on the island of Cyprus until his death. Luke chose to follow Paul as the focus of his book on the Early Church. God continued to use Paul as a pioneer with unique authority and as author of 12 New Testament letters. It never occurred to Paul or Barnabas or Mark to quit!

God has many ways to fulfill his purposes. It is wrong to think that your honest, but human, blunders can stop God's work or limit you to God's second best—whatever that is. You don't need to lose heart as long as you keep your will in tune with God. Keep right on serving God though Satan would drag out your mistakes and rehearse them in your mind. He delights in accusing the brethren! Your greatest glory does not come in never falling, but in rising every time you fall!

Marian Anderson grew up in a home financially poor, but rich in music and love and faith. When Marian was 12 years old, her father died. She began earning 50¢ or $1.00 by singing concerts at churches, YMCAs, and YWCAs. Sometimes she could sing at four or five places in one night.

After singing for a large group in Harlem, some well-meaning people decided to sponsor a concert for her in New York's Town Hall. Though it seemed incredible, Marian was not yet prepared by experience and maturity. That night at the concert hall, her sponsor delayed opening 5, 10, 15 minutes. When the curtain went up, she was horrified to see the house half-empty. Though crushed, Marian sang her heart out. When it was over, she knew she had failed. The critics agreed in the newspaper the next day. Marian Anderson was shat-

85

tered. She told her mother, "I'd better forget all about singing and do something else."

Her mother cautioned, "Why don't you think about it a little—and pray a lot—first?"

She refused to sing, avoided her music teacher, and brooded in silence—for a whole year. In those tearful hours came the realization that sometimes the most self-sufficient person cannot find enough strength to stand alone. From her torment, she prayed and poured out her heart to the Lord.

Slowly she came out of her despair. Her mind began to clear. No one needed to be blamed for her failure. Self-pity left her. With excitement she told her mother one day, "I want to study music again. I want to be the best and be loved by everyone and be perfect in everything!"

Marian's mother chided gently, "That's a wonderful goal—but our dear Lord walked this earth as the most perfect of all—yet not everybody loved Him."

One day entering the house, Marian was singing the first music she had sung in more than a year. Her mother hugged her and said, "Your prayers have been answered—and mine, too." After a moment of silence, she added, "Prayer begins where human capacity ends."

Marian Anderson made use of her mistake to become one of America's greatest concert singers. In fact, my wife and I sat enthralled with her music on Marian Anderson's Farewell Concert Tour—a musical moment to remember!

To Be Used of God

Acts 16:1-15

The way many Christians equip themselves for serving God reminds me of the small boy saying to his father, "Tomorrow I am going fishing with Bill."

Pointing to a compost pile in the yard, his father asked, "Would you like some bait, Son?"

The lad replied, "No, thanks, Dad. We don't use bait. Where we're going there aren't any fish."

God called His people to be fishers of men, but amazingly we don't go where the people are, nor do we know how to use our bait!

Though called to a life of service, many Christians pray, "Use me, Lord—especially in an advisory capacity!" While we would prefer to dictate the time and place for our service to God, we should ask with Paul, "Lord, what wilt thou have me to do?" (Acts 9:6, KJV).

After dissolving partnership with Barnabas, Paul took Silas and toured the young churches in Syria, Cilicia, and the Galatian area. "He came to Derbe and then to Lystra" (v. 1). Though Luke gives more space to pioneering churches than to the development of churches, Acts 16:1-15 portrays how God provides a place of service.

God Gives Helpers

The Lord knew the large vacancy Barnabas would leave in Paul's life. As Paul stubbornly, but sadly, walked his separate way, the Lord began providing new helpers. God knows how much we really do need each other. St. Augustine once said, "One loving heart sets another heart on fire!"

The appointment of fellow workers in the church remains under God's authority. He can bring the right ones together to do a great work for His kingdom. Silas became Paul's number one assistant. He possessed a good reputation, important ties with the apostles in Jerusalem, Roman citizenship, and the mark of God's calling upon his life.

As Paul and Silas toured Galatia, a second helper joined their group—Timothy. In Acts 14, during the first missionary journey, Paul had been dragged out of Lystra, stoned, and left for dead. One of the witnesses that day was a young boy, 14 or 15 years old, named Timothy. His mother and grandmother became Christians then. The impact of Christ was written indelibly on Timothy's heart. Now, years later, he joined Paul and was loved as a son. One day this trusted helper would receive two of Paul's most personal letters—immortalized in the New Testament for all to read.

Paul, Silas and Timothy ended up in Troas—the ancient city of Troy. There, the group is joined by the author of Acts— Luke the physician. He became the only Gentile writer of the New Testament. As Paul's helper, this historian and scholar was a bright addition.

God knows we gain insight and strength and encouragement from our coworkers and helpers. One writer commented, "Spiritual growth occurs best in a caring community. There are spiritual truths I will never grasp and Christian standards I will never attain except as I share in community with other believers—and this is God's plan. The Holy Spirit ministers to us, in large measure, through each other. This is what Paul is talking about when he says, 'We will in all things grow up into him who is the Head, that is, Christ. From him the whole body, joined and held together by every supporting ligament, grows and builds itself up in love, as each part does its work.'"[1]

Sometimes, one of us will be able to see spiritual truths and directions for Christian living when someone else cannot. Thank God, the Lord enables us to serve together—helping, encouraging, praying, caring!

At this point, Luke slips in his fourth progress report of the church: "So the churches were strengthened in the faith and grew daily in numbers" (v. 5).

God Gives Guidance

As we seek to serve God, He has promised to guide us. If we are divinely guided, we shall be divinely guarded.

"Paul and his companions traveled throughout the region of Phrygia and Galatia, having been kept by the Holy Spirit from preaching the word in the province of Asia. When they came to the border of Mysia, they tried to enter Bithynia, but the Spirit of Jesus would not allow them to. So they passed by Mysia and went down to Troas" (vv. 6-8).

God can effectively close doors. They wanted to go into the southwestern part of modern Turkey known then as Asia, but God stopped them. They wished to enter Bithynia, one of the richest provinces, but God would not let them. Paul had planned on Bithynia, but ended up in Troas! It was not his first choice.

Knowing how persistent Paul could be, I'm sure he tried hard to get into Bithynia. He never did anything halfway. But his way was blocked! His plan was broken! The Bible says, "The Spirit of Jesus would not allow them"—a vivid description of God's closed doors in life. Paul may have arrived at Troas discouraged or confused: "I wanted to go to Bithynia and here I am in Troas. What's going on?"

We don't know how God closed the doors—whether health or wealth or bureaucratic red tape or hostile people or

89

a deep inner compulsion to halt. To Paul's credit, he was sensitive enough to recognize the Spirit's restraint.

In later years, Paul would be allowed to go into those forbidden areas—but not now. God has His timing. At times God seems very slow, but we must pay attention to the Spirit's restraints. Learn to wait for God's timing. There is a certain tide of the Spirit. Don't miss it! God works to accurate timetables. Don't push ahead when the Spirit tries to check you. The Bible says, "Rest in the Lord, and wait patiently for him" (Ps. 37:7, KJV). The stops—as well as the steps—of a good man are ordered by the Lord!

Missionary Adoniram Judson faced closed doors in Burma. He suffered humiliation and disappointment. Could Judson see God's leadership? Of course not, he was human. Do you think as he lay in the emperor's prison he could always sense God's purpose? Of course not, he was human. But God eventually revealed His direction for Judson's ministry.

The famous artist, Whistler, started out as a soldier at West Point Military Academy. Unfortunately, he felt, he flunked out because he could not pass the chemistry course. He noted, "If silicon had been a gas, I should have been a major-general." Having failed, he halfheartedly attempted engineering. Almost accidentally, he tried painting and became famous. God reveals His area of service to us in many different ways.

A customs officer in Mexico was converted. When the missionary had to leave, he left the man a Bible and told him to let the Holy Spirit guide. Thirteen months later the missionary returned. The young Christian was doing fine but was puzzled. He pointed to 13 attractively bound religious books he had bought from a salesman. He said, "I started to read, but something in here (pointing to his heart) said to me, 'Don't read those books!'" They were Jehovah's Witnesses books. Though he had never heard of the cult, the Holy Spirit protected him.

90

God can effectively close doors for our own good!

When we live in the realm of the Spirit, God's "No" becomes part of His ultimate "Yes!" Learn to be grateful that God says "No" when it's for our good.

God can explicitly open doors. An old Italian proverb says, "When God shuts a door, He opens a window!" Many barriers in life have led to broader fields of service. Paul's great scheme to evangelize Bithynia fell in ruins. Paul and his companions came to Troas unemployed, frustrated, and puzzled by the closed doors all around them.

Wanting Bithynia and getting Troas! What a common experience! But Paul takes Troas—his second choice—and it became the door to greater opportunity. Though his dreams were shaken, Paul still believed God had a purpose for his life. Paul's attitude was, "If God has led me here, there is something here worthwhile to do!" God never leads a person into any place where all the doors are shut.

God can exalt second choices. God's plan is always better. God's will for your field of service is the best plan and the most effective use of your abilities, talents, and spiritual gifts. Though God's plan appears to be second choice, it has a way of being most fulfilling and exciting.

God knows where and how we can serve best. William Carey planned to go to the South Sea islands, but the Holy Spirit sent him to India. Barnado felt directed to China, but God kept him in England. Judson aimed at India, but God directed his steps to Burma.

At Troas, God began unfolding the open door of Paul's service. Out of Paul's frustrations, a dream was born! God directs our lives that way. Isaiah wrote, "Whether you turn to the right or to the left, your ears will hear a voice behind you, saying, 'This is the way; walk in it'" (30:21). That voice is usually a sense of peace, a quiet inner confirmation.

God guides us in at least five ways. First, God sometimes guides by a strong conviction or deep certainty of some spe-

91

cific assignment. Second, God sometimes guides by closing doors, by unexpected developments that hinder your immediate goal—progress suddenly blocked. Third, God sometimes guides by opening doors, providing opportunities. Fourth, God sometimes guides by His inner voice, a distinct impression or communication in the inner man. Fifth, God often guides by His voice in the Bible, His revealed Word of promise and direction.

Trusting God to guide rests on the fact that God has a wonderful plan for your life and that He will guide you to it. Theology calls that "providence." God's providence is neither fatalism nor accidentalism. Fatalism says everything has been arranged beforehand. Accidentalism says nothing is arranged beforehand. But God's providence follows His great strategy in which there's room for personal freedom and response. God's providence is flexible enough to include free moral choice and forceful enough to overrule the possibility of ultimate failure.

God's purposes do not always make themselves plain each day. Things often happen that seem to make no sense at all—to add nothing to God's ultimate plan and purpose. But keep in mind: there's more to come! The story isn't over yet! There is another chapter!

The cross of Jesus made no sense on that terrifying Friday. It took a resurrection to make sense out of it.

For Phillips Brooks, his Bithynia was a career as a college professor. Plunging into his chosen profession, Brooks failed miserably. He wrote about his students in a letter: "They are the most disagreeable set of creatures without exception that I have ever met. . . . I really am ashamed of it but I am tired, cross, and almost dead, so good night!"

After Brooks failed and dropped out of his teaching profession, he wrote, "I don't know what will become of me and I don't care much." He wanted Bithynia and got Troas. Fortunately he found God's area of service for his life. Phillips

Brooks became one of America's greatest pulpiteers. As pastor of one of Boston's historic churches, he got this cherished letter:

Dear Mr. Brooks:

I am a tailor in a little shop near your church. Whenever I have the opportunity I always go to hear you preach. Each time I hear you preach I seem to forget all about you, for you make me think of God.

Had Phillips Brooks gotten Bithynia, he would have gotten buried in academia, but through Troas came God's open door to service throughout the English-speaking world.

Many years ago a lad longed for his Bithynia as a concert musician. However, he couldn't play or sing very well. A friend named Amati, a skilled violin maker, told him, "There are many ways of making music. What matters is the song in the heart."

Arriving at his own Troas, the song of his heart was expressed. Antonio Stradivari became one of the world's greatest violin makers.

G. Campbell Morgan summed it up brilliantly: "It is better to go to Troas with God than anywhere else without Him!"

God Gives Inspiration

"So they passed by Mysia and went down to Troas. During the night Paul had a vision of a man of Macedonia standing and begging him, 'Come over to Macedonia and help us'" (vv. 8-9).

There's the inspiration of divine presence. Paul knew he had been given a vision by God. In his time of perplexity, God was near. God would enthuse him—meaning, "God in you." That's genuine inspiration. One has said, "The visions of God are only seen through the lens of a pure heart."[2] God inspires a person beyond himself.

On August 22, 1741, George Friedrich Handel shut himself into his room. Working at his desk, he labored for three weeks like a man divinely possessed. He rarely ate or slept. When he did eat, he worked with one hand and ate with the other. Though he had no commission and might never hear his composition performed, he heard a higher voice than the public. He was composing the oratorio *The Messiah.*

One day a servant found him weeping at his desk. Handel turned to him, his face shining through his tears: "I did think I did see all heaven before me, and the great God Himself!" He had just completed the "Hallelujah Chorus." Handel had the inspiration of divine presence.

In our areas of service, even in mundane tasks, God's presence is the glory of our day. He is our inspiration—God in you!

There's the inspiration of holy purpose. Suddenly Paul knew God's direction for him. As an old Quaker once said, "God can teach thee more by one flash of His light, than thou can'st learn in a lifetime without it!" It was in Troas that Paul caught a vision of an open door only 60 miles across the water—Macedonia. God's vision to Paul leaped across the straits into Greece, on to Europe, and from there around the world.

Let God's vision lift your horizons. You'll catch a glimpse of His holy purposes.

Let human need inspire you. So often when we get to our Troas, we pity ourselves. Wallowing in disappointment, we miss the vision of that man from Macedonia crying, "Come over and help us!"

Dr. Karl Menninger was asked what to do if one felt a nervous breakdown coming on. The famous psychiatrist replied, "If you feel a nervous breakdown coming on, lock up your house, go across the railroad tracks, find someone in need, and do something for him."

A young woman in New York gave up a prized position in a school attended by children of wealthy homes. She took an assignment in a squalid district on the East Side. She explained, "These East Side kids have so little. School is the one bright spot in their lives. The children in my other school had everything. They even rode to school with nurses and chauffeurs. There was no 'kick' in it for me."

Life's richest rewards, Jesus taught, are the joys from helping others.

Macartney said it eloquently: "The man from Macedonia ... wears every kind of clothing. ... Sometimes this man of Macedonia is a Greek, sometimes a Roman or a Jew or a Frenchman, a German or an Englishman, sometimes an African ... an Indian ... a Korean, a Japanese, a Chinese (even an American). ... This man from Macedonia speaks every language under the sun. But wherever and whoever he is, whatever his color and whatever his speech, there is one thing about him ... always the same—he ... needs help; he needs Christ. ... Wherever you find him, the sentence is the same: 'Come over ... and help us' (v. 9)."[3]

God Gives Ministry

God can use the person with instant obedience. "After Paul had seen the vision, we got ready at once to leave for Macedonia, concluding that God had called us to preach the gospel to them. From Troas we put out to sea and sailed straight for Samothrace, and the next day on to Neapolis. From there we traveled to Philippi, a Roman colony and the leading city of that district of Macedonia" (vv. 10-12).

The vision was neither wasted nor debated. The vision that leads to no action is not a vision—only a daydream.

The dean of the agricultural school asked the freshman, "Why have you chosen this career?"

The freshman replied, "I dream of making a million dollars in farming like my father."

The dean was impressed. "Your father made a million dollars in farming?"

"No," said the student, "but he always dreamed of it!"

95

Paul's vision moved him to action: "Immediately we endeavoured to go into Macedonia" (v. 10, KJV). As soon as daylight came, they checked passage for the first available ship to Greece. God didn't need to call twice. They were ready to obey.

A member of my church said to me, "I promised the Lord I would do the first thing I was asked to do!" He did—and God used him. God uses people who are ready to serve.

"From Troas we put out to sea and sailed straight" (v. 11). The Greek sailing term for "sailed straight" means "running with the wind." With one stop, the voyage only took two days. Later, upon their return, it took five days to sail upwind. Sometimes when we go on the King's business, the wind is with us—things go easy. But sometimes its against us—and in sailing, going upwind is more invigorating! God's timings are just right—He overcomes any circumstances that hinder.

Paul's missionary band arrived and went right to the capital city, Philippi. Twenty years after the birth of the church at Pentecost in Jerusalem, Paul took the good news of Jesus to a capital city on the European continent. Philippi stood on the site of the battle between Antony and Octavius against Brutus and Cassius. It had been founded by Philip of Macedon, father of Alexander the Great. They went right where the action is—and that continued to be Paul's philosophy of missions.

God can use the person with intentional service. Paul went there on purpose: "On the Sabbath we went outside the city gate to the river, where we expected to find a place of prayer. We sat down and began to speak to the women who had gathered there" (v. 13).

Since there were no synagogues in Philippi, when the Sabbath day came, they went down near the river. Jews often held prayer meetings near water in absence of a synagogue, since many Jewish ceremonies include rituals of washing. Paul sought out opportunities to talk about Jesus. When do you?

Too many Christians are like the fellow of whom it was said, "He served the Lord off and on for 40 years."

However, Paul the tentmaker was like William Carey of whom a friend said, "You are running around preaching, witnessing to people, and you are neglecting your shoe repair business. Don't you think you should give more time and attention to your business?"

Carey replied, "My business is extending God's kingdom. Shoe repairing just pays the expenses!"

Dr. Albert Schweitzer personified service: "I don't know what your destiny will be, but one thing I know: the only ones among you who will be really happy are those who will have sought and found how to serve!"

Of the two boys in the Taylor family, the eldest determined to make a name for his family. He became a member of the British Parliament in his quest for fame.

The younger brother followed Christ to China. Hudson Taylor, the missionary, died beloved and known on every continent. A student of history looked in the encyclopedia to see what the elder son had accomplished. He found only these words: "The brother of Hudson Taylor."

Service for Jesus makes life worth living.

God can use the person with immediate availability. "One of those listening was a woman named Lydia, a dealer in purple cloth from the city of Thyatira, who was a worshiper of God. The Lord opened her heart to respond to Paul's message. When she and the members of her houshold were baptized, she invited us to her home" (vv. 14-15). Amazingly, when Paul made himself available to God, the Holy Spirit led him right to those whose hearts were ripe and ready. God introduced him to strategic converts.

Lydia was the first Christian convert in Europe. Years later, Paul wrote to the church at Philippi from a Roman prison, "I thank my God every time I remember you. In all my prayers for all of you, I always pray with joy because of your partnership in the gospel from the first day until now" (Phil. 1:3-5). What was that first day? The day Lydia opened her heart to Jesus Christ. What a joyful occasion that was! The Philippian church became the healthiest, happiest church to whom Paul wrote. It was always his special crowning joy.

God will give each of us a ministry of joy. As we determine to serve Him, to respond with instant obedience, and to make ourselves available to Him, God will use us greatly!

A visitor who came into the sanctuary late whispered to the person in the pew beside him, "When does the service begin?"

The reply was, "Sir, the service begins as soon as the meeting ends."

Make Use of Your Detours

Acts 16:16-40

In April, a bus driver, during his first week on the job, took a wrong turn. He was appalled to find himself weaving through the city park with its budding trees and beds of blooming flowers. Though his route was an express run from the suburbs to downtown, he decided to act as if it were on purpose. He was relieved to find himself only a few minutes behind schedule.

When he pulled into the terminal, the first passenger off commented, "Young man, that was lovely! I've been riding this bus for years, and that's the first time I was treated to a free tour of the park in the springtime."

It's a mark of maturity when on a detour you can enjoy the scenery.

Life doesn't always stay on wide, easy, well-marked freeways. Unexpected detours arise in everyone's life. That gets rather confusing if you feel strongly that God has some special place or ministry or purpose for your life. How do you handle your detours?

Paul and Silas experienced a detour. After a unique vision, Paul knew God wanted him and Silas to cross over into

Europe and preach the good news about Jesus. Without hesitation, they sailed to Macedonia and traveled to Philippi.

Luke gives a firsthand account:

> One day as we were going down to the place of prayer beside the river, we met a demon-possessed slave girl who was a fortune-teller, and earned much money for her masters. She followed along behind us shouting, "These men are servants of God and they have come to tell you how to have your sins forgiven."
>
> This went on day after day until Paul, in great distress, turned and spoke to the demon within her. "I command you in the name of Jesus Christ to come out of her," he said. And instantly it left her.
>
> Her masters' hopes of wealth were now shattered; they grabbed Paul and Silas and dragged them before the judges at the marketplace.
>
> "These Jews are corrupting our city," they shouted. "They are teaching the people to do things that are against the Roman laws" *(vv. 16-21, TLB).*

Angry owners of the slave girl ranted racial prejudice, "These men are Jews" (v. 20), especially picking out Paul and Silas, most obviously Jewish members of the team. Luke was a Greek and Timothy was only half-Jewish. Two charges were leveled at them. First, "These men are Jews, and are throwing our city into an uproar" (v. 20). They were accused of creating civil disorder. The Roman Empire would not tolerate civil disturbance of public peace. Roman peace, Pax Romana, was an important principle of Roman government.

The second charge was "advocating customs unlawful for us Romans to accept or practice" (v. 21). Rome was unfriendly to new religions. Judaism had been granted legal status as a religion by Roman decree—but not Christianity. Nothing new was needed as a religion, they thought.

Luke continues his eyewitness account: "A mob was quickly formed against Paul and Silas, and the judges ordered them stripped and beaten with wooden whips. Again and again the rods slashed down across their bared backs; and afterwards they were thrown into prison. The jailer was threatened with death if they escaped, so he took no chances, but put them into the inner dungeon and clamped their feet into the stocks" (vv. 22-24, TLB).

Lictors were assistants to Roman magistrates. They carried a bundle of rods tied with leather. Often the bundle was wrapped around an axe—symbols of the legal right to inflict corporal and capital punishments. Paul and Silas were beaten with the bundle of rods. Benito Mussolini used the same kind of bundle of rods and axe as an emblem and name for his Fascist party.

A beating with a bundle of sticks tied together left a person's back a mass of bloody flesh, often causing internal hemorrhaging, damaged organs, smashed vertebrae, and broken ribs. Occasionally death followed.

The two missionaries were taken down into the inner dungeon and their legs locked in wooden stocks designed to force a prisoner's legs wide apart—a painful torture. Those lower prisons were infested with lice, rats, and disease. Prisoners were forced to exist in their own filth. Bodies throbbed with pain. They were weak from hunger, and sleep was impossible.

Obviously the glamour of God's call had dimmed. Life's difficulties come, not when God calls but when the pressure is on! I remember the night I settled God's call to preach. That was a special moment. And I recall vividly the day General Superintendent Hugh C. Benner laid his hands on my head, giving the church's official recognition of ordination. That was a high point, but there have been detours—times when it seemed I must be sidetracked from God's great purpose in my life! God's call is exciting, but He does not fill in all the blanks at the beginning.

Understandably Paul and Silas may have wondered, What in the world are we doing here? God called us to

Macedonia to preach—not get beat up and imprisoned! What's going on? God gave us a vision to come and help the people. What good can come out of being locked up?

But the devil defeats himself when he imprisons Christians. In God's economy the place of the Cross is the place of the crown! When the enemy of your soul resorts to violence, he is emptying his bag of tricks. Later Paul would write back to the Philippian church, "Now I want you to know, brothers, that what has happened to me has really served to advance the gospel" (Phil. 1:12).

Life may bring some unexpected detours. After all, through suffering we learn to mature and grow in our dependence upon God. We can benefit from our detours. How did Paul and Silas handle their detour?

Paul and Silas Prayed During Their Detour

"About midnight Paul and Silas were praying" (v. 25).

The situation looked hopeless. Darkness and prison doors seem like a final word—but God always has the last word! God is stronger than prison doors. Victor Hugo said, "There are times in a man's life when regardless of the attitude of the body, the soul is on its knees in prayer."

Paul and Silas didn't question God. They didn't lash out blaming somebody for their situation—nor did they blame each other. They didn't question God's call; they just started praying.

Luke's word for "praying" here does not carry the idea of petition or request. It indicates instead an attitude of adoration and worship. They weren't asking for anything; they were simply enjoying God's presence. Many people are like the pajama-clad child calling out to his parents, "I'm going to say my prayers. Anyone want anything?"

Paul and Silas prayed the prayer of praise and adoration to God—not asking for a thing. One preacher pointed out, "Do you remember the story of Job? He lost his investments, then his property, then his children. His wife wanted to leave him. Then his health gave out. After listing all these calamities, the Bible has a surprise line . . . packed with real meaning. It says simply, 'Then Job . . . fell down . . . and . . .' What would you think the next word would be? Cursed? Wept? Died? Wrong on all three. It says, 'Then Job . . . fell down . . . and *worshiped*' (Job 1:20)."[1]

Fellowship with God is more important than getting answers!

When you get sidelined in life, put on a shelf, or turned onto a detour, make use of it. Take the opportunity to get better acquainted with Jesus. Learn to pray in the night seasons! Regardless of how desolate your detour may seem, God has everything under control. He gets no surprises. You are *never* lost from His sight.

In your midnights, talk to God!

During the Church of the Nazarene's General Assembly of 1980, Dr. L. T. Corlett, a former president of the Nazarene Theological Seminary, spoke at the alumni banquet. Dr. Corlett sketched the precarious days during the planning and construction of the new library required for accreditation. It was an era of difficult financing. His story included several incidents of how God answered prayer at just the right time. Concluding, Dr. Corlett said, "So I took hold of my favorite Scripture: 'He thanked God, and took courage'" (Acts 28:15, KJV).

That's the way to make use of your detours!

Paul and Silas Sang Praises During Their Detour

"About midnight Paul and Silas were praying and singing hymns to God" (v. 25).

Three distinct miracles occur in this fantastic episode. The first miracle is the way Jesus Christ enabled Paul and Silas to overcome the bitterness of terrible circumstances. Their duet in the dark was not a song of deliverance but the song of contentment. Anybody can sing when prison doors are open. But the Christian can sing *in* prison. That's a different kind of song! The missionaries weren't singing to get out of jail. It was simply their choice of response to circumstances too big to handle. Rather than chafe, they chose to praise God. That kind of spirit soars even when the body is imprisoned!

Have you wondered what songs they must have sung? Most likely they sang from the Jewish hymnal, the Psalms. They might have sung Psalm 23: "The Lord is my shepherd; I shall not want. He maketh me to lie down in green pastures: he leadeth me beside the still waters. He restoreth my soul" (Ps. 23:1-3, KJV).

Perhaps Psalm 37 expressed their praises: "Fret not thyself because of evildoers . . . Trust in the Lord, and do good . . . Delight thyself also in the Lord . . . Commit thy way unto the Lord; trust also in him . . . Rest in the Lord, and wait patiently for him" (Ps. 37:1, 3-5, 7, KJV).

Surely they must have sung Psalm 46: "God is our refuge and strength, a very present help in trouble. . . . The Lord of hosts is with us; the God of Jacob is our refuge" (Ps. 46:1, 11, KJV).

The most lasting songs are born in midnights of suffering and disappointment. Songs with deep feeling and spiritual impact are hammered out on the anvil of tragedy and sorrow and are often refined in the furnace of trial and suffering. Someone wrote:

And many a rapturous ministrel among those sons of light,
Will say of his sweetest music, "I learned it in the night."
And many a rolling anthem that fills the Father's home,
Sobbed out its first rehearsal in the shade of a darkened room. [2]

Much of today's religious music will be forgotten in a few short years. The composers are sincere and devoted but have not suffered enough to give their music the ring of reality.

Much church music today lacks the depth of great praise and empathy of God's sure deliverance. There's frivolity in much of it that has no soul. No one is moved by it. Only broken hearts reach broken men and women.

Two music editors yawned over a new manuscript. One said, "I've never heard such corny lyrics, such whimpering sentimentality, such repetitious, uninspired melody. Hey, we've got a hit here!"

Eventually Paul wrote his best works from prison cells. John Bunyan's long years in the Bedford jail produced the best-seller *Pilgrim's Progress.*

From 1695 to 1705, 10 long years, Madam Guyon was locked in a French prison. Listen to the words of a song she wrote in her cell:

> *My cage confines me round;*
> *Abroad I cannot fly;*
> *But though my wing is closely bound,*
> *My heart's at liberty,*
> *My prison walls cannot control*
> *The flight, the freedom of the soul.*
>
> *Oh, it is good to soar*
> *These bolts and bars above,*
> *To Him whose purpose I adore,*
> *Whose providence I love;*
> *And in Thy mighty will to find*
> *The joy, the freedom of the mind.*

Not a song of deliverance, it's a song of contentment! She found the joy of unfettered and unbroken fellowship with the Lord.

Make use of your detours. "Sing to the Lord a new song" (Ps. 96:1). Sooner or later we are put on a night shift. Praise should not cease with the sunlight. Bishop Arthur J. Moore expressed it beautifully: "We sing a song at midnight, not because of the darkness, but because we are sure the morning will appear."

Paul and Silas Witnessed During Their Detour

"About midnight Paul and Silas were praying and singing hymns to God, and the other prisoners were listening to them" (v. 25).

The sound of singing rang through the stone-walled prison—and touched others also. As Paul and Silas continued to pray and sing, the inmates were listening—and that word *listening,* a strong word in the Greek, suggests they were listening with full attention.

Our world is always listening—Paul and Silas knew that. They weren't afraid to sing out for Jesus. Why do we who have so much to sing about express our faith so faintheartedly? The Holy Spirit wants us to sing, not to quietly mouth words. Are we afraid someone will hear us? Our timidity denies our trust in a mighty God!

Those prisoners were amazed at the contrast. Instead of groaning and whining and cursing, the duet in the darkness gave powerful, eloquent witness to God's grace. In life, our reactions are almost always more eloquent than our premeditated actions. And the people around us are always listening. We never know how our example encourages and gives hope to someone listening out there in the dark. We must ask ourselves, "Is what my family and friends see in me convincing them that Jesus is the Way?"

My mother loaned me a book that I couldn't put down until I read to the end. It's a contemporary book by Bishop Festo Kivengere titled *I Love Idi Amin.* Idi Amin has since been deposed as dictator of Uganda, but he probably has killed more Christians than any man alive today. An intriguing incident from the book reads:

In the summer of 1972, an All-East-Africa convention of the "revival brethren" was planned to be

106

held in Tanzania. These are great times of getting together—5,000, 10,000, or 25,000 people attend—and have been held in different places every year or two since about 1940. It is a wonderful thing to praise God with so many brothers and sisters, and to listen to what God is saying to us in today's circumstances.

On the day of departure, a chartered bus was at the terminal, being loaded with the Ugandan delegation to the convention. Because of the political strain between our country and Tanzania, each one had carefully gotten a permit from the Department of Military Affairs for this trip.

A crowd came down to see the travelers off. They were singing, laughing, hugging, and waving. Suddenly, up drove some army officers and a detachment of soldiers with guns and loud commands. They surrounded the whole group, delegates and friends, and marched them off to the dreaded military prison. About 80 people were jailed.

Someone had whispered a question in a high place about a large group going to the "enemy" country of Tanzania. Were they planning to join the guerillas there? Prison was the answer.

The Christians filed into the central cell of the prison in shock. There were no chairs to sit on, so in usual Ugandan style they spread out their grass mats, with which they travel, and sat on the floor. Over in one corner, someone began to sing softly: "Glory, glory, hallelujah, glory to the Lamb. . . ." Everyone picked it up, and in that moment they began to repent of their fear for their lives. The praise swelled and rolled through corridors of the most terrifying jail of Uganda, while tears of joy and release shone in the eyes of many.

Many quietly shared the change that had come to their hearts as Jesus spoke peace to them. Each one praised God.

"We thought we were going to a convention in

107

Tanzania," said one. "But we are having a convention right here!"

For two days the soldiers were exposed to the most joyous atmosphere they had ever experienced: men and women praising God that they were in prison, sharing their testimonies and the Scriptures with the soldiers, who felt loved. The soldiers' wives started slipping in to listen in amazement, too. Some soldiers went out to buy soft drinks for their new friends! A number of them came under conviction of sin and asked how they could know this Jesus, too.

Outside, the archbishop and others were busy visiting offices, explaining and showing the travel permits to the top military men and to the president, whom they finally convinced that these were loyal citizens and the trip was perfectly in order. The command was given to release them.

The soldiers and their wives lined up to shake hands with the Christians as they filed out, and they have never forgotten the love and the free spirit of these people, who knew they could lose their lives there. In fact, that year very few who had entered that prison had walked out. Most had been buried.[3]

Praise to God and a heart filled with song teach a listening world about the power of suffering love.

In that dark, lonely midnight Paul and Silas witnessed to the other prisoners by "a sacred concert . . . so successful that it brought the house down!"[4] "Suddenly there was such a violent earthquake that the foundations of the prison were shaken. At once all the prison doors flew open, and everybody's chains came loose" (v. 26). The second miracle! Earthquakes have always been common in that part of the world—but this one was special! As Stedman exclaimed, "The heart of God was so blessed . . . that He said, 'I just can't hold still; I'm going to shake the place up a bit!'"[5]

William Booth, founder of the Salvation Army, preached from this incident. After the prayers and praises of Paul and Silas, General Booth added, "And God said 'Amen!' with a mighty earthquake."

Archbishop William Temple noted, "When I pray, coincidences happen. When I stop praying, coincidences stop happening."

Chaplain Johnson went on a bombing raid with his men. Returning after a successful mission, the plane suddenly sputtered and the engines failed—out of gas. They glided to a safe landing on an island in Japanese-infested territory.

The staff sergeant said, "Chaplain, you've been telling us about the need to pray and believe God to answer in time of trouble. Here's your chance to prove what you've been preaching. We're out of gas and our base is several hundred miles away. We are surrounded by the enemy."

The chaplain began to pray, claiming the promises of God. He believed God would work a miracle somehow. He prayed all afternoon. While the crew slept that night, he continued in prayer. About two o'clock in the morning, the staff sergeant awakened, walked to the water's edge and found a metal flat which had drifted up on the beach—a barge with 50 barrels of high-octane gasoline.

In a few hours the crew was safely back at the base. It turned out that the skipper of a United States' tanker, finding his ship in submarine-infested waters, removed his gasoline cargo to eliminate the danger of a torpedo hit. Barrels were put on barges and set adrift 600 miles from where Chaplain Johnson and his men were forced down. God brought one barge through wind and currents and beached it 50 steps from the stranded crew.

The more we pray and praise God, the more "coincidences" will happen. The more we start praising God, other people listening in will be set free. When we start praising God, people will begin to loosen up and find the joyful liberty in Christ. One fellow testified, "The greatest jailbreak that ever occurred was when Jesus Christ set me free from the prison of sin!"

Paul and Silas, though free to escape, continued to witness for the Lord in their difficult detour.

> The jailer woke up, and when he saw the prison doors open, he drew his sword and was about to kill himself because he thought the prisoners had escaped. But Paul shouted, "Don't harm yourself! We are all here!"
>
> The jailer called for lights, rushed in and fell trembling before Paul and Silas. He then brought them out and asked, "Sirs, what must I do to be saved?"
>
> They replied, "Believe in the Lord Jesus, and you will be saved—you and your household." Then they spoke the word of the Lord to him and to all the others in his house. At that hour of the night the jailer took them and washed their wounds; then immediately he and all his family were baptized. The jailer brought them into his house and set a meal before them; he was filled with joy because he had come to believe in God—he and his whole family (vv. 27-34).

The missionaries refused to exercise their freedom at another person's expense—what a contrast to today's value system of "doing your own thing!" From a human perspective, they owed the jailer nothing. After their terrible beating, he had put them into the lowest prison, unnecessarily adding the torture of the stocks. Without emotion, without one thought for their suffering, he went right to sleep! It wasn't his business to worry about their comfort—only to be sure they did not escape. Human kindness was missing.

When he realized they had voluntarily spared his life—the price of allowing a prisoner to escape—he cried out, "Sirs, what must I do to be saved" (v. 30). That is a universal question, and the answer must not contain anything a man couldn't do if he were dying!

Those missionaries gave the jailer a solid, adequate answer: "Believe in the Lord Jesus, and you will be saved" (v. 31). In the Greek text the jailer asks, *"Lords,* what must I do to be saved?" He knew they were special, so he addressed them with the title of respect, conscious that he was in the presence of superiors.

However, they replied, "Believe in the *Lord* Jesus." "You have called us 'lords.' We are not your answer. Believe in the *Lord* Jesus. He is the only *Lord* of life!"

Rosalind Rinker wrote, "The reason we do not have confidence when we witness to our faith is that we think it's up to us. It is never up to us! When we make this plain, the other party is relieved, and so are we! Then God can get on with His own persuading without having us get in His way."

What kind of answer would we have given the jailer? Try harder? Help your fellowman? Join a church? Get religion? Keep the Golden Rule? The only adequate answer is "Believe in the Lord Jesus!"

Stuart Briscoe visited a church where a man had been assigned to escort him as a host. Briscoe said, "He told me about the history of the church, the building problems, and the leaky roof. Then he moved on to the organist, the choir, and the choir director. This led naturally to the minister and his predecessor. . . . Then he gave me a brief account of the history of each family in the church. But gradually he began to run out of material. Naturally I felt I ought to help as I asked him, 'And what about the Lord Jesus?' If I had kicked him he couldn't have looked more startled. He didn't answer me. With a desperate look at his watch, he headed for the door muttering. . . . He was a man with a life-long time of service in that church; his mind was steeped in its traditions and history. His life revolved around its activities, and his mouth spoke out of the abundance of his heart. But his heart had nothing

111

to abound about as far as the Lord was concerned, so his lips were silent concerning Him."[6]

William Barclay noted, "First and foremost, a witness . . . knows the facts . . . first hand. If ever you have to be a witness in a law court, the judge will never allow you to repeat what someone else told you; he will compel you to stick to what you know and have seen and have heard yourself. To be a witness is to . . . [have] first-hand knowledge . . . to be able to say . . . 'This is true and I know it.'"[7]

As a result of witnessing to the jailer on their detour, the third miracle occurred—the miracle of a changed nature! After Paul and Silas explained the "word of the Lord," Luke says, "At that hour of the night the jailer took them and washed their wounds" (v. 33). There were two washings that night—first when the jailer cleansed their wounds; second when the captives baptized the jailer symbolizing a life made clean.

"The jailer . . . set a meal before them" (v. 34). Literally, "He spread a table before them." That's what God does: "Thou preparest a table before me in the presence of mine enemies" (Ps. 23:5, KJV). The great miracle was not the earthquake; it was belief in Jesus Christ, so that the very life of God possessed the jailer's heart.

When life forces you into detours, keep on praying, keep on singing praise to God, and keep on witnessing—others are listening. God can use you to change lives. Make use of your detours! The Bible says, "Blessed is the man who perseveres under trial, because when he has stood the test, he will receive the crown of life that God has promised to those who love him" (James 1:12).

Joseph was a stranger in the foreign land of Egypt—but God used him to save his people. Esther was queen in a land that hated her people—but God used her there to save her people. Daniel was jailed in a den of lions—but God needed him there as a witness to God's power and grace. Paul and

112

Silas suffered in the Philippian jail—but God used them to lead a jailer and his family to Jesus.

Why has God placed you where you are at this moment?

Notes

Chapter 1

1. Ray C. Stedman, *Growth of the Body* (Santa Ana, Calif.: Vision House Publishers, 1976), 11-12.

2. J. Oswald Sanders, *On to Maturity* (Chicago: Moody Press, 1962), 199.

3. William P. Barker, *They Stood Boldly* (Westwood, N.J.: Fleming H. Revell Co., 1967), 104.

4. Jerry Cook, *Love, Acceptance, and Forgiveness* (Glendale, Calif.: Regal Books, a division of G/L Publications, 1979), 67.

Chapter 2

1. Charles R. Hembree, *Fruits of the Spirit* (Grand Rapids: Baker Book House, 1969), 89.

2. Clyde M. Narramore, *This Way to Happiness* (Grand Rapids: Zondervan Publishing House, 1958), 52.

Chapter 3

1. Joseph H. Mayfield and Ralph Earle, *Beacon Bible Commentary,* Vol. 7 (Kansas City: Beacon Hill Press of Kansas City, 1965), 418.

2. Cook, *Love, Acceptance, and Forgiveness,* 55.

3. Ibid., 11.

4. Floyd Thatcher, *The Miracle of Easter* (Waco, Tex.: Word Books, Publishers, 1980), 137.

5. W. T. Purkiser, *When You Get to the End of Yourself* (Kansas City: Beacon Hill Press of Kansas City, 1970), 16.

Chapter 4

1. William Sanford LaSor, *Great Personalities of the New Testament* (Westwood, N.J.: Fleming H. Revell Co., 1961), 11.

2. Lloyd John Ogilvie, *Drumbeat of Love* (Waco, Tex.: Word Books, Publishers, 1976), 193.

3. Idea suggested by Dr. Frank G. Carver in an unidentified magazine article.

4. Stedman, *Growth of the Body,* 63.

5. Ogilvie, *Drumbeat of Love,* 196.

6. Source unknown.

Chapter 5

1. Mildred Bangs Wynkoop, *A Theology of Love* (Kansas City: Beacon Hill Press of Kansas City, 1972), 225.

2. D. James Kennedy, *Evangelism Explosion* (Wheaton, Ill.: Tyndale House Publishers, 1970), 101.

Chapter 6

1. Ogilvie, *Drumbeat of Love,* 193.

2. Ibid., 196.

3. Ibid., 197.

4. Wynkoop, *Theology of Love,* 25.

5. Ogilvie, *Drumbeat of Love,* 193.

6. Cook, *Love, Acceptance, and Forgiveness,* 13.

7. Henry Jacobsen, *The Acts Then and Now* (Wheaton, Ill.: Victor Books, a division of SP Publications, 1973), 118-19.

8. Ibid., 126.

Chapter 7

1. *Los Angeles Times,* 1980.

2. Stedman, *Growth of the Body,* 76.

3. Curtis Vaughan, *Acts: A Study Guide* (Grand Rapids: Zondervan Publishing House, 1974), 110.

4. William S. Deal, *Problems of the Spirit-filled Life* (Kansas City: Beacon Hill Press of Kansas City, 1965), 68.

5. William L. Coleman, "The Value of Falling on Your Face," *Eternity,* Sept. 1974, 23.

6. Ibid., 75.

7. Ogilvie, *Drumbeat of Love,* 198.

8. Deal, *Problems of the Spirit-filled Life,* 68.

Chapter 8

1. Howard A. Snyder, *The Community of the King* (Downers Grove, Ill.: InterVarsity Press, 1978), 75.

2. John D. Drysdale, *The Price of Revival* (Liverpool: C. Tinling and Co., 1946), 19.

3. Clarence Edward Macartney, *Macartney's Illustrations* (New York: Abingdon-Cokesbury Press, 1949), 236.

Chapter 9

1. William P. Barker, *Saints in Aprons and Overalls* (Westwood, N.J.: Fleming H. Revell, Co., 1959), 47-48.

2. Source unknown.

3. Bishop Festo Kivengere, *I Love Idi Amin* (Old Tappan, N.J.: Fleming H. Revell Co., 1977), 20-21.

4. Stedman, *Growth of the Body,* 92-93.

5. Ibid., 95.

6. Stuart Briscoe, *Living Dangerously* (Grand Rapids: Zondervan Publishing House, 1968), 54.

7. William Barclay, *God's Young Church* (Philadelphia: Westminster Press, 1970), 76.

Bibliography

Airhart, Arnold E. *Beacon Bible Expositions.* Vol. 5, *Acts.* Kansas City: Beacon Hill Press of Kansas City, 1977.

Alford, Henry. *The New Testament for English Readers.* Chicago: Moody Press, n.d.

Asch, Sholem. *The Apostle.* Translated by Maurice Samuel. New York: G. P. Putnam's Sons, 1943.

Banks, Louis Albert. *Paul and His Friends.* New York: Funk and Wagnalls Co., 1898.

Barclay, William. *God's Young Church.* Philadelphia: Westminster Press, 1970.

———. *The Acts of the Apostles; The Daily Study Bible.* Philadelphia: Westminster Press, 1953.

Barker, William P. *Saints in Aprons and Overalls.* Westwood, N.J.: Fleming H. Revell Co., 1959.

———. *They Stood Boldly.* Westwood, N.J.: Fleming H. Revell Co., 1967.

Benson, Joseph. *Benson's Commentary,* Vol. 4. New York: T. Mason and G. Lane, 1839.

Blaikie, William G. *A Manual of Bible History.* New York: Ronald Press Co., 1940.

Blair, Edward P. *The Acts and Apocalyptic Literature.* New York: Abingdon-Cokesbury Press, 1946.

Briscoe, Stuart. *Living Dangerously.* Grand Rapids: Zondervan Publishing House, 1968.

Bruce, F. F. "Commentary on the Book of the Acts." *The New International Commentary on the New Testament.* Grand Rapids: Wm. B. Eerdmans Publishing Co., 1976.

———. *New Testament History.* Garden City, N.Y.: Doubleday and Co., 1971.

Buttrick, George Arthur, editor. *The Interpreter's Bible.* Vol. 9. New York: Abingdon Press, 1954.

Carter, Charles W., and Earle, Ralph. *The Evangelical Commentary on the Acts of the Apostles.* Grand Rapids: Zondervan Publishing House, 1959.

Carver, William Owen. *The Acts of the Apostles.* Nashville: Broadman Press, 1916.

Clarke, Adam. *Clarke's Commentary.* Vol. 5. New York: Abingdon Press, n.d.

Coleman, William L. "The Value of Falling on Your Face." *Eternity,* September, 1974.

Cook, Jerry. *Love, Acceptance, and Forgiveness.* Glendale, Calif.: Regal Books, a division of G/L Publications, 1979.

Davidson, F., editor. *The New Bible Commentary.* Grand Rapids: Wm. B. Eerdmans Publishing Co., 1958.

Davies, G. Henton; Richardson, Allen; and Wallis, Charles L., editors. *Twentieth Century Bible Commentary.* New York: Harper and Brothers, Publishers, 1955.

Deal, William S. *Problems of the Spirit-filled Life.* Kansas City: Beacon Hill Press of Kansas City, 1965.

DeHaan, M. R. *Pentecost and After.* Grand Rapids: Zondervan Publishing House, 1964.

Demaray, Donald E. *The Book of Acts.* Grand Rapids: Baker Book House, 1959.

Drysdale, John D. *The Price of Revival.* Liverpool: C. Tinling and Co., 1946.

Ellicott, Charles John, editor. *A Bible Commentary for English Readers,* Vol. 7. London: Cassell and Co., n.d.

Fallis, William J. *Studies in Acts.* Nashville: Broadman Press, 1949.

Halley, Henry H. *Bible Handbook.* Grand Rapids: Zondervan Publishing House, 1959.

Hembree, Charles R. *Fruits of the Spirit.* Grand Rapids: Baker Book House, 1969.

Henry, Carl F. H., editor. *The Biblical Expositor.* Vol. 3. Philadelphia: A. J. Holman Co., 1960.

Henry, Matthew. *Matthew Henry's Commentary on the Whole Bible.* Edited by Leslie F. Church. Grand Rapids: Zondervan Publishing House, 1961.

Hervey, A. C. "The Acts of the Apostles." *The Pulpit Commentary,* Vol. 1. Edited by H. D. M. Spence and Joseph S. Exell. London: Funk and Wagnalls Co., 1908.

Jacobsen, Henry. *The Acts Then and Now.* Wheaton, Ill.: Victor Books, a division of SP Publications, 1973.

Kennedy, D. James. *Evangelism Explosion.* Wheaton, Ill.: Tyndale House Publishers, 1970.

Kingsley, Florence Morse. *Paul: A Herald of the Cross.* Philadelphia: Henry Altemus, 1898.

Kivengere, Bishop Festo. *I Love Idi Amin.* Old Tappan, N.J.: Fleming H. Revell Co., 1977.

LaSor, William Sanford. *Church Alive.* Glendale, Calif.: Regal Books, a division of G/L Publications, 1972.

118

————. *Great Personalities of the New Testament.* Westwood, N.J.: Fleming H. Revell Co., 1961.

Lenski, R. C. H. *The Interpretation of the Acts of the Apostles.* Minneapolis: Augsburg Publishing House, 1961.

Macartney, Clarence Edward. *Macartney's Illustrations.* New York: Abingdon-Cokesbury Press, 1949.

Mayfield, Joseph H., and Earle, Ralph. *Beacon Bible Commentary.* Vol. 7, *John; Acts.* Kansas City: Beacon Hill Press of Kansas City, 1965.

Morgan, G. Campbell. *An Exposition of the Whole Bible.* Westwood, N.J.: Fleming H. Revell Co., 1959.

————. *The Acts of the Apostles.* Westwood, N.J.: Fleming H. Revell Co., 1924.

Narramore, Clyde M. *This Way to Happiness.* Grand Rapids: Zondervan Publishing House, 1958.

Ogilvie, Lloyd John. *Drumbeat of Love.* Waco, Tex.: Word Books, Publishers, 1976.

Pfeiffer, Charles F. *Baker's Bible Atlas.* Grand Rapids: Baker Book House, 1961.

Pfeiffer, Charles F., and Harrison, Everett F., editors. *The Wycliffe Bible Commentary.* Chicago: Moody Press, 1962.

Purkiser, W. T. *When You Get to the End of Yourself.* Kansas City: Beacon Hill Press of Kansas City, 1970.

Robertson, Archibald Thomas. *Word Pictures in the New Testament.* Vol. 3, Nashville: Broadman Press, 1930.

Sanders, J. Oswald. *On to Maturity.* Chicago: Moody Press, 1962.

Snyder, Howard A. *The Community of the King.* Downers Grove, Ill.: InterVarsity Press, 1978.

Spence, H. D. M., and Exell, Joseph S., editors. *The Acts of the Apostles.* Vol. 2, *The Pulpit Commentary.* London: Funk and Wagnalls Co., 1908.

Stedman, Ray C. *Growth of the Body.* Santa Ana, Calif.: Vision House Publishers, 1976.

Stirling, John F. *An Atlas Illustration of the Acts of the Apostles and the Epistles.* New York: Fleming H. Revell Co., n.d.

Taylor, Kenneth. *The Living Bible.* Wheaton, Ill.: Tyndale House Publishers, 1971.

Thatcher, Floyd. *The Miracle of Easter.* Waco, Tex.: Word Books, Publishers, 1980.

Thomas, W. H. Griffith. *Outline Studies in the Acts of the Apostles.* Grand Rapids: Wm. B. Eerdmans Publishing Co., 1956.

Unger, Merrill F. *Unger's Bible Handbook.* Chicago: Moody Press, 1967.

Vaughn, Curtis. *Acts: A Study Guide.* Grand Rapids: Zondervan Publishing House, 1974.

Wynkoop, Mildred Bangs. *A Theology of Love.* Kansas City: Beacon Hill Press of Kansas City, 1972.